Spanish and Portuguese Jews

in the

Caribbean and the Guianas

FIG. 1. The Jewish Savanna in 1839, with a view of the synagogue, in a photograph of a contemporary painting by the Belgian artist Pierre Jacques Benoit (1782-1854). Courtesy of the Museum of History, Paramaribo, Suriname.

Spanish and Portuguese Jews in the Caribbean and the Guianas

A Bibliography

Compiled by
MORDECHAI ARBELL

Edited for the
John Carter Brown Library
by
Dennis C. Landis and Ann P. Barry

THE JOHN CARTER BROWN LIBRARY
Providence, Rhode Island
and
INTERAMERICAS
New York, New York

Inquiries concerning this work should be directed to The John Carter Brown Library, Box 1894, Providence, Rhode Island 02912 or visit www.JCBL.org.

The John Carter Brown Library is an independently funded and administered institution for advanced research in history and the humanities located at Brown University since 1904. In order to facilitate and encourage use of the Library's outstanding collection of printed and manuscript materials concerning the Americas from 1493 to ca. 1825, the Library offers fellowships, sponsors lectures and conferences, regularly mounts exhibitions for the public, and publishes catalogues, bibliographies, facsimiles, and other works that interpret the Library's holdings.

InterAmericas®/Society of Arts and Letters of the Americas/*Sociedad de Artes y Letras de las Américas*, a program of the New York Foundation for the Arts, was created in 1992 to provide both funding and a venue for programs that celebrate the richness and diversity of the arts and humanities in the Americas. Correspondence should be addressed to InterAmericas, 162 East 78th Street, New York, N.Y. 10021, e-mail: ia1992@artswire.org.

Copyright 1999 by the John Carter Brown Library

This work may not be reproduced in whole or part, in any form or medium, for any purpose, without prior permission from the copyright owner.

ISBN 0-916617-52-1

Contents

LIST OF ILLUSTRATIONS vii

FOREWORD *by Norman Fiering* ix

INTRODUCTION *by Mordechai Arbell* xiii

EDITORIAL PREFACE *by Dennis C. Landis* xix

ABBREVIATIONS USED IN THE BIBLIOGRAPHY xxiii

I.	Suriname, Guiana, Tobago, Cayenne 1
II.	Netherlands Antilles: Curaçao 23
III.	Netherlands Antilles: St. Eustatius, Aruba, St. Maarten 31
IV.	Barbados 37
V.	Jamaica 45
VI.	The Virgin Islands: St. Thomas and St. Croix, and the Island of Nevis 55
VII.	Colombia and Venezuela 61
VIII.	Panama, El Salvador, Costa Rica, Belize 69
IX.	Dominican Republic 73
X.	Haiti, Martinique, Guadeloupe 75
XI.	Trinidad 81
XII.	General 83

INDEXES

Author/Title 109
Subject 147
Places 159

List of Illustrations

Fig. 1   The Jewish Savanna in 1839 .... Frontispiece

Fig. 2   Remnants of the synagogue *Beraka ve Shalom* in Suriname 3

Fig. 3   The synagogue *Neve Shalom* in Paramaribo, Suriname 7

Fig. 4   The sand-covered floor of the synagogue *Neve Shalom* 15

Fig. 5   Detail from the tombstone of David Senior, 1749 25

Fig. 6   Ruins of the synagogue *Honen Dalim* in St. Eustatius 33

Fig. 7   The marble laver at the synagogue *Nidhei Israel* in Bridgetown, Barbados 39

Fig. 8   The decanter given to Moses Delgado 47

Fig. 9   The Spanish-Portuguese Jewish cemetery in Barranquilla, Colombia 63

Fig. 10 The Spanish-Portuguese Jewish cemetery in Coro, Venezuela 64

Foreword

In the public mind, "history" and "the past" are often treated as though they were equivalent, but a little consideration makes clear that the past is the infinite, undifferentiated sum of all that has occurred, whereas history has to be extracted from this sum to become intelligible and meaningful. We say casually that this or that person "made history" by some action, but it is not the action that makes the history so much as the person who writes about the action.

It is in the latter sense that Mordechai Arbell is a true maker of history, and his achievement is the outgrowth of a particular passion. He has devoted a good part of his life to uncovering and documenting the elusive story of the Jews who populated, in small numbers, the southern New World empires of the Spanish, the Portuguese, the French, the Dutch, and the English, often covertly, and always quietly. At a young age Arbell was a diplomat in the Israeli foreign service. Among numerous posts, he was assigned for a time as Consul in Bogota, as Ambassador to Panama, and as Ambassador to Haiti. Conspicuous as he would be in all of those places as the representative of a "Jewish" country, the history of Jews in South America and the Caribbean at first was simply *presented* to him by people living there, descendants of Jewish colonists who recalled their heritage.

Later Mr. Arbell entered the corporate world, which still required of him much foreign travel, while at the same time his research interest in this fugitive history became deeper and more earnest. Of Sephardic origins himself, the study of the Spanish- and Portuguese-speaking Jews of the Caribbean basin was, in some respects, an extension of his own history. Early in the 1980s, Mr. Arbell began to lecture and publish on the subject of the "Spanish-Portuguese Jewish Nation of the Carribbean"—"nation" being the contemporary term—and after so many years of concentrated study (not to speak of on-site field work at jungle-covered Jewish cemeteries and ruins of synagogues), he is recognized today worldwide as an incomparable source of information on this subject.

The present compilation—based on a manuscript completed by Mr. Arbell in 1996 and only now published—is a cumulative record of his bibliographical gleanings over thirty years. It is the kind of bibliography that one could hardly set out to compile systematically. It is too full of dispersed data found in obscure and ephemeral journals. Much of what is offered here had to be discovered by serendipity. It will prove to be a marvelously useful work, although the reader should know that it reveals only the dry bones of Mr. Arbell's research, not the learning and enthusiasm that characterizes his lecturing and his substantive writing.

For the John Carter Brown Library, the appearance of this bibliography complements perfectly, and not by accident, the publication early in 2000 of a collection of essays on a closely related subject, *The Jews and the Expansion of Europe, 1450 to 1800*, edited by Paolo Bernardini (New York and Oxford: Berghahn Books), a work to which Mr. Arbell is a contributor. There the reader will find a good example of Mr. Arbell's skill as a historian as well as several other essays that relate specifically to the Caribbean and Suriname. The twenty-five essays in that collection were derived directly from a conference at the Library in 1997.

Bibliographies, to serve their purpose, must be as accurate and complete as we can make them. When Mr. Arbell delivered his manuscript to us, we did not worry about its completeness, because no bibliography is exhaustive, and in

Foreword

any case, enough time had already been devoted to the accumulation of the information. On the other hand, we did feel that it was necessary to attend to minor inconsistencies and technical errors that had crept into the manuscript in the course of so many years of gathering the data. Dennis C. Landis, the Curator of European Books at the Library, had just completed his six-volume *European Americana: A Chronological Guide to Works Printed in Europe Relating to the Americas, 1493-1750*, and happily was available to serve as the Library's in-house editor of the Arbell bibliography. He recruited Ann Phelps Barry—formerly assistant editor on the *European Americana* project—to help him, and together they worked to ensure that the mechanics of the bibliography were reasonably sound. Dr. Landis and Ms. Barry made the citations more uniform, and added key elements when they were missing. They assessed the work from a librarian's point of view, anticipating that the listings, many of them obscure, will generate not only visits to the stacks but also numerous interlibrary loan requests, which must be absolutely precise if one is to get a positive result.

In the area of Jewish studies relating to the Americas during the colonial period, the John Carter Brown Library has been privileged to have the collaboration in the past decade of the Touro National Heritage Trust. Mordechai Arbell was a Touro Fellow at the JCB in 1993, at a time when this fellowship was supported by annual grants from the Trust. In the past year the Trust, with the cooperation of the Dorot Foundation, has been able to endow this fellowship in perpetuity. Thus, there will always be modest funds at the JCB to underwrite research on the Jewish experience in this hemisphere from its earliest beginnings to ca. 1825.

Most important in connection with this book—and in fact much else in the Library's work since 1993—has been the generosity of Mrs. Jane Gregory Rubin and the entities she represents, InterAmericas and the Reed Foundation.

Mrs. Rubin serves brilliantly on the Library's Board of Governors and in general is a creative force in all that we do. It is a pleasure to acknowledge here her help as well as the help of Mr. Bernard Bell, the president of the Touro Trust.

The John Carter Brown Library is dedicated to the study of the Americas during the colonial period, i.e., the study of this hemisphere during the era of European involvement in American affairs, which ended in the 1820s with the revolutions for independence in Spanish and Portuguese America. The Library is not focused on any particular aspect of this history—whatever happened between Hudson Bay and Patagonia is grist for the mill, keeping in mind, however, that "history" is always selective, a search for meaning and significance. We avidly collect the primary sources needed for research in this period, and sponsor research through fellowships, conferences, publications, and other means, looking for areas of study that are perhaps somewhat neglected or marginalized. The actions and experiences of the Jews in this place and era—both observant Jews and Christianized Jews—interconnects with major elements of the story of the early Americas. This book, we trust, will help to make that case.

Norman Fiering
Director and Librarian
John Carter Brown Library

Introduction

For the past thirty years I have been studying the history of Jewish settlement in the Caribbean and the Guianas, a process that began as early as the middle of the seventeenth century. As I conducted my research, I made copious bibliographical notes on the books, articles, and other printed material that I encountered, read, and studied.

No comprehensive bibliography in this area of interest existed, and it was apparent to me, as I worked, that what I had found would be invaluable to my successors. It was during my stay as a Touro National Heritage Trust Fellow at the John Carter Brown Library in Providence, Rhode Island, and following my visits to the Research Institute for the Study of Man and InterAmericas in New York, that I decided to collect into a usable list all of the printed material known to me on the subject.

The Caribbean region and the Guianas were the area of colonial infighting among the European powers—mainly Britain, France, the United Provinces of the Netherlands, Denmark, Sweden, Latvia, Spain, and Portugal. The Jewish population, the majority of which was of Spanish-Portuguese origin, lived under various Protestant regimes (being excluded from Spanish and Portuguese colonies owing to persecution by the Catholic Inquisition, and being expelled from French possessions by the Black Code in force from 1685).

As a result of these circumstances, books on the Jewish history in the area were written in English, Dutch, French, and Danish, or if by Jewish settlers, in Hebrew, Spanish, or Portuguese, mainly in the early years of settlement. These books were published either in the capitals of the colonial powers—London, Paris, The Hague, or Amsterdam—or in the colonies themselves, mainly in Paramaribo, Suriname; Willemstad, Curaçao; Kingston, Jamaica; Bridgetown, Barbados; Charlotte Amalie, St. Thomas, Virgin Islands; and Georgetown, Guyana. In a more recent period (the early years of the 19th century), after the settlement of the Caribbean Jews in the newly liberated Spanish colonies or in the United States, books on the subject were published in Spanish in Caracas, Bogota, Panama City, San José, and Santo Domingo, and in English in the United States.

The books, articles, and monographs included in this bibliography either deal specifically with Jewish settlement and life, or are narratives by explorers, diaries of missionaries, soldiers, or governors, or general history books that refer to the Jewish history in the area. Unpublished doctoral theses and dissertations are also included, since they can be located in university libraries.

The bibliography is divided by geographical area, citing printed material dealing specifically with a given area, and also contains a final, general chapter which includes works on the Jewish history of the region as a whole. The areas specified are:

1) <u>Suriname, Guiana, Cayenne, and Tobago</u>. The area of settlement of the Jews in the so-called "Wild Coast"—which included the colonies of Cayenne, Suriname, Demerara, Berbice, Essequibo, and Pomeroon—was passed from hand-to-hand among the British, French, and Dutch. The area includes as well the island of Tobago, the history of which is intimately connected with the Wild Coast, serving as an outpost for shipping to and

to and from the region, and which was ruled, in different periods, by the Dutch, British, French, and Latvians.

2) Curaçao in the Netherlands Antilles. An island with a rich cultural and religious Jewish history that has served, and still serves, as the Jewish center of the Caribbean.

3) St. Eustatius, Aruba, and St. Maarten in the Netherlands Antilles. An area where Jewish life had begun by the early eighteenth century and may be characterized as of a commercial nature as opposed to the plantation economy of the Wild Coast.

4) Barbados. An island with Jewish life distinct from other islands, one on which Jews lived in a hostile social environment and in constant struggle for equal rights.

5) Jamaica. An island settled by *conversos* under Spanish rule and which had at least twelve Jewish communities after occupation by the British.

6) The Virgin Islands (St. Thomas and St. Croix) and Nevis. In this chapter are books dealing with the second wave of Jewish settlement to the Virgin Islands, mainly from the island of St. Eustatius after its destruction, and to the island of Nevis, with Jewish settlers coming from Barbados.

7) Colombia and Venezuela. The two countries in which, after their liberation from Spain, Jews settled, especially in Barranquilla and Riohacha in Colombia, and in Coro and Barcelona in Venezuela.

8) Panama, El Salvador, Costa Rica, Belize. The countries in which Caribbean Jews settled at a later stage.

9) <u>Dominican Republic</u>. One of the few countries in which Jews lived under Spanish rule, mainly as Dutch or British subjects.

10) <u>Haiti, Martinique, Guadeloupe</u>. Books describing the short period of Jewish life in the French colonies, until the expulsion of the Jews in 1685, and the limited Jewish life there afterwards.

11) <u>Trinidad</u>. An island where Jewish life started after the British occupation, but in which the Jewish population was always small.

12) <u>General</u>. In this concluding chapter are books dealing with Jewish history in the Caribbean and the Guianas as a whole, without specifically relating to a country or an island; books dealing with Dutch Brazil and its Jewish population, which are relevant to the settlement of the Caribbean and the Guianas; books dealing with the *converso* settlements in Spanish America, which had connections with the Jews of the Caribbean; and works on the early settlement in the United States directly relating to the settlement of Caribbean Jews there.

Despite all the efforts made to have the bibliography as comprehensive as possible, some printed works may have been missed, since no project of this kind can be complete. There will always be room for additions. I can only hope that future researchers will find this work helpful and that it will increase interest in a history that richly deserves treatment.

Acknowledgments

Numerous people have helped me prepare this bibliography. I will mention only a few of them. Prof. Gerard Nahon of the Sorbonne in Paris for his encouragement and advice; the late Rabbi Malcolm Stern and the late Earl (Alvin)

Introduction

Fidanque who pushed me to continue my research on the Caribbean and the Guianas; Dr. Norman Fiering, the director of the John Carter Brown Library, and the Library staff, who helped locate a large part of the items listed in this bibliography, and particularly Dr. Dennis Landis and Ms. Ann Phelps Barry, who helped to lift this bibliography to a higher level; Jane Gregory Rubin, director of InterAmericas, and Prof. Lambros Comitas, director of the Research Institute for the Study of Man (RISM), and the librarian and staff of RISM for their encouragement and useful ideas; Mr. Ainsley Henriques in Jamaica; Dr. Abraham Peck of the American Jewish Archives, Cincinnati; Mrs. Odette Vlessing of the Municipal Archives in Amsterdam; Dr. Avi Beker, director of the World Jewish Congress in Jerusalem, for his support and encouragement; Mr. Hatal of the Ben-Zvi Institute in Jerusalem, for his invaluable assistance; Mrs. Fern Seckbach for her help in writing, styling, copyediting, and indexing the bibliography; and last but not least, my wife, sons, and daughters-in-law for their patience and helping hands. Thank you all.

Mordechai Arbell

Tel Aviv, Israel
1996

Editorial Preface

In the years since 1977, the assembling of bibliographical data for the *European Americana* series (The John Carter Brown Library and Readex Books, 1980-1997) has led to an enhanced understanding of numerous constituent topics that define this vast field of literature. One of the emerging topics within this information matrix was "Judaica Americana," a concept that, arguably, encompasses three distinct subjects: books on Jews *in* the Americas, writings by Jews *about* the Americas, and Jewish topics that fall under discussion within volumes understood to be "Americana" for other reasons. From our perspective, the topic of Judaica Americana is quite old, probably beginning with the *converso* interpreter, learned in Hebrew, taken on Columbus's first voyage. It also includes such important early books as Abraham Farissol's 1586 Hebrew treatise that helped propagate Vespucci's New World observations. For a variety of reasons—above all a sparse knowledge of Hebrew among bibliographers of Americana—the books belonging to this topic form a field still to be properly delineated.

The scope of the current work by Mordechai Arbell, focused on the Caribbean and the Guianas, and including manuscripts and many modern journal articles, is of course quite different from that of *European Americana*, which concludes with European books printed in 1750. There is very little overlap between the two bibliographies; indeed, when Mr. Arbell came to Providence for research in 1993, the editors shared their files with him and found that they had nothing to offer that he had not already identified as germane to his project.

When Mr. Arbell at last presented his completed draft bibliography to the John Carter Brown Library in 1996, we were impressed by the breadth of its coverage and the wealth of resources that had been collected. The Library seized the opportunity to bring this work to publication, not merely as a tribute to Mr. Arbell's decades of research and the scope of his erudition, but because the bibliography met a clearly perceived need. The preparations for our 1997 conference, "The Jews and the Expansion of Europe to the West," made manifest the importance of Spanish and Portuguese Jews to the processes of colonization and trade in the Caribbean and coastal Latin America. At the same time, it was apparent that the bibliographical resources needed to pursue research topics in this area were widely dispersed and inaccessible through any central listing.

Mr. Arbell's citations were gathered in the course of thirty years as an adjunct of his own research. It was our belief, upon examining the manuscript, that the user of the printed bibliography would be best served if, first of all, the entries were reviewed by the editors as to regularity of citation form. We also took care to add any important elements that might not have been recorded in the original citation. Further, we believed the work should be reviewed from a reference librarian's point of view, since we anticipate that the listings presented here will propel interested scholars into both their own institutional libraries and more distant repositories, as well as generating many interlibrary transfer requests, an increasingly automated, sensitive procedure.

Having undertaken the task of revising the bibliography and preparing it for publication, the present editors were mindful of the pressure of time, and necessarily limited the scope of this editorial project. For example, no attempt was made to regularize the capitalization of titles according to differing national conventions, and diacritical marks—largely absent from the manuscript—have not generally

Editorial Preface

been added. The editing process made use chiefly of data from online library catalogues for verification purposes, and did not utilize the more detailed paper resources which would have enlarged the scope of the effort. It was not possible, nor would it have been prudent, to verify every citation. Ann Phelps Barry was particularly helpful to the process through her familiarity with online resources, her eye for consistency, and her linguistic expertise.

Authorship conventions in the bibliography have largely been revised to conform to North American library practice; however, Mr. Arbell has been able, through his extensive travels and use of informal information networks, to establish authorship for various fugitive publications for which authorship had not previously been known to cataloguers. Where Mr. Arbell's personal familiarity with a family and the way its members use their surname differs from North American library practice, we have given the former preference, and provided a cross-reference from the standardized usage in the author-title index. Similarly, the name given alphabetical prominence in some cases is the suppressed Sephardic Jewish name rather than the Christian surname (e.g., Levi de Barrios rather than Barrios); a cross reference is given in the index.

In the text of the bibliography, author names are given in boldface type, except in cross-references. Book titles (in italics) are occasionally the main filing point for a work, where the identification of an author or editor is impractical. An article from a journal or other collection is given in quotation marks. When several publications by an author appear in the same chapter, these are arranged chronologically. Whenever possible, place names are given in the citations of serials; these are often invaluable for the identification of obscure journals and newspapers.

Entries for manuscripts are given in quotation marks. Mr. Arbell has cited locations for each manuscript listed, and in the case of manuscripts in his own possession, has kindly consented to provide copies for reading at the John Carter Brown Library.

The author-title index is intended as a quick finding list for the works listed in the twelve chapters. Authors appear in boldface type, book titles in italics, articles and manuscripts within quotation marks. Title listings in the index frequently omit the initial article.

Mr. Arbell has himself stated that this work will not contain every conceivable article and book relating to his subject. Further relevant material has undoubtedly come to light since his closing date of 1996 for coverage. It is our institutional aspiration that the John Carter Brown Library might serve as a clearing-house and repository for such information, with the intention of an eventual supplementary publication. Indeed, visiting scholars such as Jonathan Schorsch—a JCB research fellow in 1998—have already demonstrated much enthusiasm about contributing to the effort of amassing such material. In this way, the documentation of this absorbing subject will become ever richer.

Dennis C. Landis
Curator of European Books
John Carter Brown Library

Abbreviations

AJA	*American Jewish Archives*
AJH	*American Jewish History*
AJHQ	*American Jewish Historical Quarterly*
JSS	*Jewish Social Studies*
MGWJ	*Monatsschrift für Geschichte und Wissenschaft des Judentums*
NHCS	*Nevis Historical and Cultural Society*
PAJHS	*Publications of the American Jewish Historical Society*
TJHSE	*Transactions of the Jewish Historical Society of England*
WIG	*De West-Indische Gids*

Spanish and Portuguese Jews

in the

Caribbean and the Guianas

I

Suriname, Guiana, Tobago, Cayenne

[1] **Mordehay Arbel.** "Los Sefaradis de Pauroma," *Aki Yerushalayim* (Jerusalem), no. 21, anyo 6 (Apr. 1984): 11–12.

Notes on the Jewish settlement in Pomeroon, today the Republic of Guyana.

[2] **Mordehay Arbell.** "Los Sefaradis i el dezvelopamiento agrikolo-ekonomiko de Sud-Amerika," *Aki Yerushalayim* (Jerusalem), no. 43, anyo 12 (1991): 14–15.

Notes on the agro-industries developed by the Jews on the South American coasts.

[3] **Mordechai Arbell.** "The Failure of the Jewish Settlement in the Island of Tobago," in *Proceedings of the Eleventh World Congress of Jewish Studies* (Jerusalem, 1994), 302–11.

A description of the short-lived Jewish settlement in Tobago, and the reasons for its failure.

[4] **Mordechai Arbell** and **Barouh Lionarons.** "Jerusalem aan de Suriname rivier. Pioniers hunkerend naar Heilige Land," *Sim Shalom* (Paramaribo), 3:4 (1992): 11–14.

Expression of the deep feelings held by the Jews of Suriname during the early settlement regarding the Holy Land and Jerusalem.

[4a] **Joao Lucio d'Azevedo.** "Judeus de Surinam," in his *Historia dos Christaos Novos Portugueses* (Lisbon, 1921), pp. 494–96.

Report by a Portuguese ambassador on a special mission in 1797 to meet the Portuguese Jews of Suriname.

[5] **Eveline Bakker, Leo Dulhuisen,** and **Mauritz Massankhan.** *Geschiedenis van Suriname.* Paramaribo, 1993. 176 pp.

Description of plantations, slavery, and everyday life in Suriname and of the Jewish involvement in it.

[6] **Mario Barata.** "A Nacao Judaica Portuguesa do Surinam a e sua relacoes com o Brazil no seculo XVIII," *Comentario* (Rio de Janeiro), 1 (1960): 54–57.

On the special connection between the Jews of Suriname and the Portuguese authorities in Brazil, and on the 18th-century Portuguese authorities' change of attitude towards the Jews who had escaped Portugal in the 16th and 17th centuries.

[7] [Not used; see no. 20a.]

[8] [Not used; see no. 61a.]

[9] **Jacques Nicolas Bellin.** *Description Geographique de la Guyane. Contenant les Possessions et les Etablissemens des Francois, des Espagnols, des Portugais, des Hollandois dans ces vastes Pays.* Paris, 1763. 294 pp.

A first-hand description of the settlement of the coast of the Guianas and (briefly) the life of the Jews there. This title is that of the engraved title page; the printed t.p. has the spelling "Guiane".

[10] **Ralph G. Bennett.** "The Jews of Exotic Surinam and Their History," *Los Muestros* (Brussels), Dec. 1992: 6–7.

[11] **Antoine Biet.** *Voyage de la France equinoxiale en l'isle de Cayenne entrepris par les Francois en l'annee M.DC.LII.* Paris, 1664. 432 pp.

A detailed description of life in the French possessions in the 1650s and the attitude toward Jews before their expulsion from them. The book also contains an eyewitness account of the Jewish market in Martinique.

[12] **R. Bijlsma.** "De stichting van de Portugeesch-Joodsche gemeente en Synagoge in Suriname," *WIG* (Amsterdam), 2 (1920): 58–61.

A documented study of the synagogues in Suriname during the first years of settlement there.

[13] **R. Bijlsma.** "De Brieven van Gouverneur van Aerssen van Sommelsdijk," *WIG* (Amsterdam), 1923: 436–38.

In one of the first letters by the first Dutch Governor of Suriname, a positive opinion on the Jewish settlers in Suriname.

[13a] **R. Bijlsma.** "David de Is. C. Nassy, Author of the *Essai Historique sur Surinam*," in Robert Cohen, ed., *The Jewish Nation in Surinam* (Amsterdam, 1982), pp. 65–73.

FIG. 2. Remnants of the synagogue *Beraka ve Shalom* founded in 1685, in the so-called "Jerusalem on the riverside" in the "Jewish Savanna" of Suriname.

About one of the most prominent Surinamese Jews, tracing his career, achievements, and important literary role.

[14] **Harry Bloch.** "David D'Isaac Nassy, M.D., 1748(?) to 1806 — First Jewish Physician in Philadelphia," *New York State Journal of Medicine* (New York), 77 (Apr. 1977): 807–809.

Account of the Surinamese merchant and apothecary who also became a respected physician in Philadelphia and returned to Suriname as a leader of the Jewish community.

[15] **Günter Böhm.** "The Synagogues of Surinam," *Journal of Jewish Art* (Chicago), 6 (1978): 98–104.

A description of the synagogues of Paramaribo and the Jewish Savanna.

[16] **Henry Bolingbroke.** *A Voyage to the Demerary, containing a Statistical Account of the Settlements There, and of Those on the Essequebo, the Berbice, and other contiguous Rivers of Guyana.* London, 1809. 220 pp.

Narrative of a voyage to what was British Guiana, describing social discrimination against the Jews by the Dutch and including a description of the remains of the destroyed Pomeroon settlement. First published in London, 1807; other editions: Philadelphia, 1813, and Georgetown, British Guiana, 1947.

[17] **J. A. Bueno de Mesquita** and **Fred. Oudschans Dentz.** *Geschiedkundige tijdtafel van Suriname . . . aanvangende met het jaar 1613 tot en met het jaar 1924.* Paramaribo, 1925.

A chronology of events in Suriname.

[18] **Louis Cardozo de Bethencourt.** "Notes on the Spanish and Portuguese Jews in the United States, Guiana, and the Dutch and British West Indies during the Seventeenth and Eighteenth Centuries," *PAJHS*, 29 (1929): 7–38. (Surinam, 14–19; Tobago, 37.)

A historical article based on documents, including those from the Jewish settlements in Suriname and Tobago.

[19] **Gertrude Carmichael.** *The History of the West Indian Islands of Trinidad and Tobago.* London, 1961. 463 pp.

A comprehensive history of the islands of Trinidad and Tobago.

[20] **Liliane Chauleau.** *Tobago et la presence francaise.* Fort de France: Archives Departmentales de la Martinique, 1992. 30 pp.

A description of French intentions for making Tobago their colony.

[20a] **Jean de Clodore.** *Relation de ce qui s'est passe dans les Isles et Terre Ferme de l'Amerique, pendant la derniere Guerre avec l'Angleterre et depuis, en execution du Traite de Breda avec un journal du dernier voyage du Sr de la Barre en la Terre Ferme et l'Isle de Cayenne.* Paris, 1671. Vol. 1, 386 pp.; vol. 2, 494 pp.

A historical account of, and diary by, the emissary of the King of France to Guiana and Martinique, describing the prohibition against exercising the Jewish religion.

[21] **Robert Cohen.** "New Aspects of the Egerton Manuscript," (Jerusalem, 1970). Manuscript in the Library of Dutch Jewish History, Hebrew University of Jerusalem.

Analysis of the manuscript found in the Egerton Collection in the British Library concerning Jewish rights on the Wild Coast.

[22] **Robert Cohen.** "Passage to a New World: The Sephardi Poor of 18th Century Amsterdam," in *Neveh Ya'akov: Jubilee Volume presented to Dr. Jaap Meijer on the occasion of his seventieth birthday* (Assen, 1982), pp. 31–42.

Shows how the Sephardic communal leaders of Amsterdam dealt with the Jewish poor by shipping them to the colony of Suriname.

[23] **Robert Cohen.** "A Mis-Dated Ketuba: A Note on the Beginnings of the Surinam Jewish Community," *AJA* (Cincinnati), 36 (1984): 13–15.

Examination of the controversy over the exact date of the beginning of Jewish settlement in Suriname.

[24] **Robert Cohen.** *Jews in Another Environment, Surinam in the Second Half of the Eighteenth Century.* Leiden & New York, 1991. 350 pp.

The single best English-language study of Surinamese Jewry.

[25] **Robert Cohen,** ed. *The Jewish Nation in Surinam: Historical Essays.* Amsterdam, 1982. 103 pp.

A collection of essays by different authors on various aspects of Jewish life in Suriname; the items include: R. A. J. van Lier, "The Jewish Community in Surinam: A Historical Survey" (no. 69b, below); L. L. E. Rens, "Analysis of Annals relating to Early Jewish Settlement in Surinam" (cf. no. 101); G. W. van der Meiden, "Governor Mauricius and the Political Rights of the Surinam Jews" (no. 73a); J. A. Schiltkamp, "Jewish Jurators in Surinam"; R. Bijlsma, "David de Is. C. Nassy"; and others.

[26] **Nellis Crouse.** *The French Struggle for the West Indies 1665–1713.* New York, 1943. 313 pp.

A description of French efforts to settle different islands in the Caribbean.

[27] **Rini S. C. Da Costa.** "De Kweekschool op de Joden Savanne" (Paramaribo, 1956). 3 pp. Manuscript in the possession of M. Arbell.

A study on the efforts to maintain Jewish education in the Jewish Savanna.

[28] **Rini S. C. Da Costa.** "De Geneeskrachtige Bron van de Joden Savanne" (Paramaribo, 1956). 27 pp. Manuscript in the possession of M. Arbell.

[29] **Rini S. C. Da Costa.** "Joden Savanne: een historische plaats in het oerwoud van Suriname," *Suralco Magazine* (Paramaribo), 1973: 21–29.

Description of the Jewish Savanna in 1973.

[30] **Rini S. C. Da Costa.** "De Gebeurtenissen in deze Eeuw op Jodensavanne" (Paramaribo, 1992). 5 pp. Manuscript in the possession of M. Arbell.

20th-century events in the Jewish Savanna.

[31] **N. Darnell Davis.** "The Beginnings of British Guiana," *Timehri* (Demerara), 7 (1893): 137–39.

The early history of Western Guiana (now the Republic of Guyana).

[32] [Not used; see no. 4a.]

[33] **Lucile D. Deen.** "Anglo-Dutch Relations from 1660 to 1688." Ph.D. thesis, Radcliffe College, 1936.

On the complicated relations between the British and the Dutch in the second half of the 17th century, ranging from friendship to armed competition.

FIG. 3. The synagogue *Neve Shalom* in Paramaribo, Suriname, founded in 1735.

[34]   [Not used; see nos. 47a and 47b.]

[35]

[36]   **David de Sola Pool.** "The Mohelim of Curaçao and Surinam," *PAJHS*, 25 (1917): 138–41.

[37]   **Hendrick Willem Dornsberg** and **Cornelius Dornsberg.** *Beschrijving van de Plechtigheden nevens de Lofdichten en Gebeden, uitgesproken op het eerste Jubelfeest van de Synagogue der Portugeesche Joodsche Gemeente, op de Savane in de Colonie Suriname, genaamd Zegen en Vrede.* Amsterdam, 1785. 47 pp.

The ceremonies celebrating the hundredth anniversary of the construction of the "Beraka ve Shalom" synagogue in the Jewish Savanna in Suriname.

[37a]   **Jean Baptiste Dutertre.** *Histoire Generale des Antilles Habitees par les Francois.* Paris, 1667–71. Vol. I, 591 pp.; vol. II, 525 pp.; vol. III, 357 pp.; vol. IV, 362 pp.

Historical narratives by a French ecclesiastic in which there are descriptions of the Jews' activities in French colonies after the Jews' expulsion from Dutch Brazil. An eyewitness account of the Jews' landing in Martinique and of their production of cocoa.

[38]   **George Edmonton.** "The Dutch in Western Guiana," *English Historical Review* (London), 16 (1901): 642–51.

History of the periods of Dutch occupation in what is today the Republic of Guyana.

[39]   *Encyclopedie van Suriname.* Amsterdam, 1977. 716 pp.

The encyclopedia contains numerous items on the Jewish settlement and life in Suriname and Jewish individuals there.

[40]   **G. J. Fabius.** "Het leenstelsel van de West Indische Compagnie," *Bijdragen Koninklijk Instituut voor de Tropen* (Amsterdam), LXX (1915): 555–594.

On the Dutch West India Company, its activities, interests, and management, including the Jewish settlement under its auspices.

[41]   **B. Felsenthal and Richard Gottheil.** "Chronological Sketch of the History of the Jews in Surinam," *PAJHS*, 4 (1896): 1–8.

A calendar of the main events pertaining to the Jews of Suriname.

[42] **Haim Finkel.** "Two Ancient Maps Illustrating the Early History of the Jews of Surinam," *Sefunim: Bulletin of the National Maritime Museum* (Haifa), 6 (1981): 81–92.

Maps showing the sites of the first Jewish settlements in Suriname in the mid-17th century.

[43] **Jos Fontaine.** *Uit Suriname's Historie.* Zutphen, 1980. 192 pp.

An illustrated history of Suriname which includes the Jewish presence there. Text in Dutch and English.

[44] **Joseph Gompers.** "The First Settling of Jews in Surinam, Pathetic History of the Plight of Some of Our Little Known Brethren," *The American Hebrew* (New York), Jan. 1930: 321–56.

On the difficulties encountered by the first Jewish settlers in Suriname.

[45] **Cornelis Ch. Goslinga.** *The First Colonization of Tobago by the Courlanders and the Dutch.* Museum of Tobago History, Publication no. 7. Scarborough, 1978. 10 pp.

On the attempts at colonizing Tobago by the Latvian Courlanders and the Dutch Lampsins brothers, and the conflict between them.

[46] **Richard Gottheil.** "Contributions to the History of the Jews in Surinam," *PAJHS*, 9 (1901): 129–42.

Important notes, based on archival documents, on Jewish settlement in Suriname.

[47] **Richard Gottheil.** "Dr. David Nassy in Surinam," *PAJHS*, 9 (1901): 143–44.

Description of a 1797 letter of appreciation by the Portuguese government to Dr. David Nassy and the Suriname Jewish community for their kindness to Portuguese sailors in distress.

[47a] **Silvia W. de Groot.** "Pierre Jacques Benoit in Surinam," *Surinam Airways Magazine* (Paramaribo), 1977: 2–25.

On the Belgian painter Benoit (1782–1854) who has left us the best paintings existing today of the Jewish Savanna as it appeared in the early 19th century, as well as material on life in Suriname in general.

[47b] **Silvia W. de Groot.** "Summary with Annotations" [in English], in Pierre Jacques Benoit, *Reis door Suriname: Beschrijving van de*

Nederlandse bezittingen in Guyana (Zutphen, 1980), pp. 85-99. (Added title page in English: *Journey through Suriname: Description of the possessions of the Netherlands in Guiana. Adapted from: Voyage a Surinam.*)

In addition to the summary of Benoit's text, this volume includes many reproductions of his paintings, among which are some of the Jewish Savanna.

[48]   **J. H. J. Hamelberg.** *Tobago. Een vergeten Nederlandsche Kolonie.* Willemstad, Curaçao, 1900.

History of the Dutch settlement in Tobago.

[49]   **V. T. Harlow, ed.** *Colonising Expeditions to the West Indies and Guiana, 1623–1667.* London, 1925. 262 pp.

Narratives on colonizing expeditions, including a description of Jews from Brazil founding a colony on the Baromia River (Pomeroon), and the text of the agreement between the British and the Dutch maintaining Jewish rights.

[50]   **Jan Jacob Hartsinck.** *Beschryving van Guiana, of de Wilde Kust, in Zuid-America . . . Essequebo, Demerary, Berbice, Suriname.* Amsterdam, 1770. 2 vols., 976 pp.

A classic work on the Dutch occupation of the colonies on the Wild Coast that often includes the full texts of relevant documents, among them some dealing with the Jewish population. Texts are not always identical with versions found in the Dutch archives.

[51]   **P. A. Hilfman.** "Notes on the History of the Jews in Surinam," *PAJHS* (Waltham), 18 (1909): 179–207.

Analysis of some documents relevant to Jewish history in Suriname.

[52]   **H. Hoetink.** "The Dutch Caribbean and Its Metropolis," in E. J. De Kadt, ed., *Patterns of Foreign Influence in the Caribbean* (Oxford, 1972), pp. 103–20.

A section of the article deals with the strong Jewish influence on life in the Caribbean.

[53]   **J. H. Hollander.** "Documents Relating to the Attempted Departure of the Jews from Surinam 1675," *PAJHS*, 6 (1907): 9–29.

Documents describing the controversial attempt of Jews to leave Suriname with the British, upon the arrival of the Dutch.

[54] **Meir Kayserling.** "Die Juden in Surinam," *MGWJ*, 8 (1859): 205–13.

Short notes on the Jewish community in Suriname.

[55] **C. K. Kesler.** "Tobago. Een vergeten Nederlandsche Kolonie," *WIG* (Amsterdam), 10 (1928): 527–34.

History of the Dutch settlement in Tobago.

[56] **M. R. Khudabux.** "The Excavation of Skeletal Material at Joden Savanne," in *Stichting Surinaams Museum,* no. 41 (Paramaribo, 1983), pp. 19–26.

Report on research carried out on the Jewish graves in the Jewish Savanna during the military regime in Suriname, 1983, which led to the destruction of sections of the old gravestones.

[57] **J. Kleyntjens.** "De Koerlandse Kolonisatiepogingen op Tobago," *WIG*, 30 (1949): 193–216.

Description of the Latvian settlement in Tobago.

[58] **Ewald von Klopmann.** "Abrege de l'histoire de Tobago," *WIG*, 30 (1949): 197–216.

History of the competition between colonial powers for a foothold in Tobago. Part of the preceding article, no. 57.

[59] **C. Koeman, ed., with F. C. Bubberman, A. H. Loor, B. Nelemans, G. Schilder, and J. B. Ch. Wekker.** *Links with the Past. The History of the Cartography of Suriname 1500–1971.* Amsterdam, 1973. 177 pp.

A compilation of the cartographic history of Suriname, containing 39 maps from the 16th, 17th, 18th, and 19th centuries, with their description, history, and background. Some of them have details on Jewish plantations, the names of the owners, and the holdings' Hebrew Biblical names.

[60] **George Alexander Kohut.** "Who Was the First Rabbi of Surinam?" *PAJHS*, 5 (1897): 119–24.

A study of the first years of a Jewish community in the Jewish Savanna.

[61]   **M. Kopuit.** "Joden-Savanne in Suriname worde nationaal monument," *Elseviers Weekblad van Zatertag* (Amsterdam), 18 Mar. 1961, pp. 7–9.

A short description of the Jewish Savanna in Surinam.

[61a]   **Antoine Joseph Le Febvre de La Barre.** *Description de la France Equinoctiale cy-devant appellee Guyanne et par les Espagnoles El Dorado.* Paris, 1666. 52 pp.

A report on the status of the French colony in Guiana, providing also a population estimate for the Jewish settlement in Remire (p. 40).

[62]   **Jean Baptiste Labat.** *Nouveau Voyage aux Isles de l'Amerique.* Paris, 1722. Vol. I, 532 pp.; vol. II, 598 pp.; vol. III, 549 pp.; vol. IV, 558 pp.; vol. V, 524 pp.; vol. VI, 514 pp.

A detailed, impressive description by a French ecclesiastic, Labat, of his voyages in the Caribbean and the Guianas, with an account of Jewish production of cocoa and vanilla.

[63]   **Jean Baptiste Labat.** *Voyage du Chevalier des Marchais en Guinee, Isles Voisines et a Cayenne fait en 1725.* Amsterdam, 1731. Vol. I, 335 pp.; vol. II, 242 pp.; vol. III, 307 pp.; vol. IV, 392 pp.

The description of various voyages and visits to Africa and America, including first-hand information on the settlement of Jews from Brazil on the island of Cayenne.

[64]   **Manfred Lehmann.** "Some Tombstones from the Joden Savanne in Surinam," in *Dutch Jewish History: proceedings of the fifth [i.e., 6th] Symposium on the History of the Jews in the Netherlands, Jerusalem, November 25–28, 1991* (Jerusalem, 1993), p. 32.

[65]   **Manfred Lehmann.** "Prominent Religious Leaders in the Joden Savanna in Surinam" Paper submitted to the 6th International Symposium on the History of the Jews in the Netherlands, Jerusalem, 1991. Manuscript in the Library of Dutch Jewish History, at the Hebrew University of Jerusalem.

The story of some Jewish religious leaders in Suriname.

[66]   **Manfred Lehmann.** "בקור בסורינם" ("Visit to Surinam"), in his *Masot u-Masa'ot* (Jerusalem: Rav Kook Institute, 1982), pp. 259–72.

Impression of a 1960 visit to Jewish sites in Surinam.

[67] **Daniel Levi de Barrios.** "Triumphal carro de la Perfeccion por el Camino de la Salvacion," in his *Triumpho del Govierno Popular* (Amsterdam, 1701), pp. 631–35.

A poem mentioning the death of the poet Levi de Barrios' wife in Tobago.

[68] [Not used; see no. 100a.]

[69] **Lou Lichtveld.** *A Valuable document concerning Tobago — 1647.* Mount Irvine Museum Trust Publication No. 2. Scarborough, 1977. 6 pp.

Document elucidating the disturbed history of Tobago.

[69a] **Rudolf van Lier.** *Samenleving in een grensgebied.* The Hague, 1949.

A historical study of the social structure of Suriname.

[69b] **Rudolf van Lier.** "The Jewish Community in Surinam: a Historical Survey," in Robert Cohen, ed., *The Jewish Nation in Surinam* (Amsterdam, 1982), pp. 19–27.

[70] **Zvi Loker.** "An Eighteenth-Century Prayer of the Jews of Surinam," in Robert Cohen, ed., *The Jewish Nation in Surinam* (Amsterdam, 1982), p. 75–87.

The prayer was to be said on going out to fight the rebel Maroons (Bush Negroes).

[71] **Zvi Loker.** "קאיין—פרק בהגירה ובהתיישבות יהודית בעולם החדש במאה הי'ד (גילויים חדשים)" ("Cayenne — A Chapter of Jewish Immigration and Settlement in the New World in the 17th Century — New Discoveries"), *Zion* (Jerusalem), 48a (1983): 107–16.

Additional documents on the history of the Jewish settlement in Remire, Cayenne, offering insight into the Jews' life there.

[72] **Zvi Loker.** "Les Juifs a Cayenne," in *La Grande Encyclopedie de la Caraibe* ([Italy:] Sanoli, 1990), vol. 7 (Histoire de la Guyane), pp. 22–27.

History of the Jewish settlement in Remire (Irmire) on the island of Cayenne.

[73] **Zvi Loker.** "On the Jewish Colony at Remire, French Guyana," in *Proceedings of the Tenth World Congress of Jewish Studies*, Division B, vol. II (Jerusalem, 1990), pp. 467–72 (also in *Judaica Latinoamericana*, 2 (1993), pp. 9–16).

A study on the Jewish settlement in Remire, Cayenne, when still in Dutch hands.

[73a] **G. W. van der Meiden.** "Governor Mauricius and the Political Rights of the Surinam Jews," in Robert Cohen, ed., *The Jewish Nation in Surinam* (Amsterdam, 1982), pp. 49–56.

A description of the governorship of Jan Jacob Mauricius (1742–1751), his positive attitude toward Jewish settlers, and his treatment of disputes within the Jewish community.

[74] **J. Meijer.** *Pioneers of Pauroma — Earliest History of the Jewish Colonization of America.* Paramaribo, 1954. 55 pp.

Analysis of a rare document describing a voyage of Jewish settlers from the Netherlands to Pomeroon in Guyana.

[75] **J. Meijer.** *Van Corantijn tot Marowijne, Beknopt Overzicht van de Geschiedenis van Suriname.* Paramaribo, 1956. 56 pp.

History of the settlement of Suriname, its minorities and different religions.

[76] **J. Meijer.** *M. J. Lewenstein's Opperrabinaat te Paramaribo (1857/8–1864): Analyse van het Surinaamse Jodendom in zijn Crisisperiode.* Amsterdam, 1959. 138 pp.

Life in Suriname's Jewish community in the 19th century, and the unification of the Portuguese and Ashkenazi communities.

[77] **H. P. Mendes.** "Privileges Granted by the British Government to the Jews of Surinam, 1665," *PAJHS*, 9 (1901): 144–46.

Record of the privileges granted the Jews of Suriname by the British, quite exceptional for the British territories at that time.

[78] **W. R. Menkman.** "Suriname in Willoughby's Tijd," *WIG* (Amsterdam), 26 (1944/5): 1–18.

Suriname under British rule.

[79] **Benjamin S. Mitrasingh.** "Archeological Investigation at Joden Savanne — A Preliminary Report," in *Stichting Surinaams Museum*, no. 41 (Paramaribo, 1983), pp. 4–8.

Report of the archeological research in the Jewish Savanna during the military regime in Suriname, 1983, which left the site of the old Jewish cemetery damaged.

FIG. 4. The sand-covered floor of the synagogue *Neve Shalom* in Paramaribo, Suriname. Photograph by Micha Bar-Am, in the Arbell Collection, Museum of the Jewish Diaspora, Tel-Aviv.

[80] **Yitzhak R. Molho.** "El poeta y dramaturgo Michael de Barrios," *Tesoro de los Judios Sefardies* (Jerusalem), 7 (1964): 99–100.

An essay on the poet Daniel Levi de Barrios; it mentions his effort at settling in Tobago.

[81] **Brian Moore.** *Race, Power and Social Segmentation in Colonial Society — Guyana after Slavery, 1838–1891.* New York, 1987. Vol. 4 of series: Caribbean Studies.

Study of race relations in colonial times in what is now the Republic of Guyana.

[82] **Henk Morroy.** *Drie Eeuwen Jodendom in Suriname: expositie in het Mahamad Ned. Isr. Synagoge . . . 2 t/m 23 augustus 1992.* Paramaribo: 1992. 6 pp.

Short description of the Jewish history of Suriname.

[83] **Gerard Nahon.** *Les "Nations" Juives Portugaises du Sud-Ouest de la France (1684–1791).* Paris, 1981. 511 pp.

A collection of historical documents on Portuguese Jewish history in southwest France, one of which shows that there was a tendency to send Jewish "vagabonds" from France to Suriname.

[84] **David de Isaac Cohen Nassy.** *Essai Historique sur la Colonie de Surinam: sa fondation, ses revolutions, ses progres, depuis son origine jusqu'a nos jours.* Paramaribo, 1788 (reprinted Paramaribo, 1968). Vol I, 192 pp.; vol. II, 197 pp.

A Jewish leader of 18th-century Suriname describing the Jewish settlement there, its problems and relations with the authorities. Dedication and preface signed variously: Mos. Pa. de Leon, Saml. H. de la Parra, Ishak de la Parra, David de Is. C. Nassy, Samuel H. Brandon, David N. Monsanto, J. H. de Barrios, Jr. Most scholars view Nassy as the sole or principal author of this work. At the very least, however, he consulted with the other signatories in the development of the text. It is the view of this compiler that the *Essai historique* should be considered a work of collective authorship by the undersigned Surinamese Jewish leaders.

[84a] **David de Isaac Cohen Nassy.** *Historical essay on the colony of Surinam,* 1788. (Papers of the American Jewish Archives, no. 8.) New York and Cincinnati, 1974. 258 pp.

A translation of no. 84.

[85] **Pieter Martinus Netscher.** *Geschiedenis van de Kolonien Essequebo, Demerary, en Berbice, van de vestiging der Nederlanders aldaar tot op onzen tijd.* The Hague, 1888. 356 pp.

A comprehensive history of the Dutch colonies in Western Guiana up to the final British occupation.

[86] **Gert Oostindie.** "Synagogen aan de Wilde Kust," NRC *(Nieuwe Rotterdamse Courant),* 4 Apr. 1992, pp. 2–4.

[87] **J. D. Oppenheim.** "Jewish Customs among the Suriname (Dutch Guiana) Population," *Edoth* (Jerusalem), 3 (1947–48): LXV–LXXV (English), 78-87 (Hebrew).

The impact of the Jewish settlers on the local population of Suriname, who adopted some Jewish customs.

[88] **Samuel Oppenheim.** "An Early Jewish Colony in Western Guiana and Its Relation to the Jews in Surinam, Cayenne and Tobago," *PAJHS,* 16 (1907): 95–186, 209–220.

A tightly detailed and documented article on the Jewish colony of New Zealand in Pomeroon, Western Guiana, and the Jewish settlements in Cayenne, Suriname, and Tobago.

[89] **Samuel Oppenheim.** *An Early Jewish Colony in Western Guiana, 1658–1666, and Its Relation to the Jews in Surinam, Cayenne and Tobago.* New York, 1907.

A reprint of no. 88.

[90] **Samuel Oppenheim.** "An Early Jewish Colony in Western Guiana: supplemental data," *PAJHS,* 17 (1909): 53–70.

Supplemental data, found mainly in the West India Company archives in the Hague and Amsterdam, on Jews in Western Guiana.

[91] **Samuel Oppenheim.** "A Letter of David Nassy of Surinam," *PAJHS,* 23 (1915): 185–86.

David Nassy, a Surinamese physician in Philadelphia, writes about human rights in the U.S.A., and in Pennsylvania in particular.

[91a] **Fred. Oudschans Dentz.** *De Kolonisatie van de Portugeesch Joodsche natie in Suriname en de geschiedenis van de Joden Savanne.* Amsterdam, 1975. 63 pp.

History of the Jewish settlement in Suriname, including a list of gravestones in the Jewish Savanna. Originally published in 1927.

[92] **Fred. Oudschans Dentz.** "De kolonisatie van Guiana," *WIG* (Amsterdam), 25 (1943): 248–54.

A description of the settlement of the Dutch in Suriname and Guyana, in which Jews played an important part.

[93] **Fred. Oudschans Dentz.** "Wat er overbleef van het Kerkhof en de Synagoge van de Joden-Savanne in Suriname," *WIG* (Amsterdam), 29 (1948): 210–34.

Description of the Jewish Savanna, its Jewish cemetery, and a list of epitaphs found there. Unfortunately, those in Hebrew are not included.

[94] **Fred. Oudschans Dentz.** "Joodse Kleuringen in Surinam," *WIG* (Amsterdam), 35 (1955): 234.

Notes on the Jewish community of color in Paramaribo, "Darkei Yesharim," which existed until the beginning of the 19th century.

[95] **Fred. Oudschans Dentz.** "The Name of the Country Surinam as a Family Name," *PAJHS*, 48 (1958–59): 19–27, 262–64.

The history of the Surinamer family, a Jewish family that traveled to Indonesia, keeping 'Surinam' in the family name.

[96] **Fred. Oudschans Dentz.** "Wat er overbleef van het kerkhof en de Synagoge van de Joden Savanne in Suriname," *WIG* (Amsterdam), 42 (1962): 210–16.

Notes on the Jewish sites in the Jewish Savanna in Suriname.

[97] [Not used; see no. 91a.]

[98] **Wilhelmina Christina Pieterse.** *Daniel Levi de Barrios als Geschiedschrijver van de Portuguees-Israelietische gemeente te Amsterdam in Zijn "Triumpho del Govierno Popular".* Amsterdam, 1968. 211 pp.

A book based on the writings of Daniel Levi de Barrios, mentioning his family's stay in Tobago and Martinique.

[99] **Pierre Pluchon, ed.** *Histoire des Antilles et de la Guyane.* Toulouse, 1982. 476 pp.

A history of the settlement of the Caribbean and the Guianas.

[99a] "Rapport van de Colonie Essequibo en Demerary" [1790?]. 131 pp. Manuscript in the John Carter Brown Library.

Report by two 18th-century Dutch special commissioners on circumstances in the colony, including some Jewish problems.

[100] **D. Regeling.** "De Joden in Suriname," *Onze Eeuw* (Amsterdam), 12 (1920): 84–104.

[100a] *Relation de la prise des Isles de Goree au Cap-Vert et de Tabago dans l'Amerique sur les Hollandois, par l'escadre de Vaisseaux du Roy, commandee par le Comte d'Estrees, Vice-Admiral de France, avec le particularitez de la prise du Fort d'Orange, et de la ruine des habitations appartenant aux Hollandois, sur la riviere d'Ouyapogue, par le Chevalier de Lezi, gouverneur de la Cayenne.* Paris, 1678. 11 pp.

Report on the fleet of d'Estrees during Oct.-Dec. 1677, at war with the Dutch, and the first days of French rule. Cyprien Lefebvre de Lezy was French governor of Cayenne.

[101] **L. L. E. Rens.** "Analysis of Annals Relating to the Early Jewish Settlement in Surinam," *Vox Guyanae* (Paramaribo), 1 (1954): 19–38.

A critical article on the histories previously written about the Jews of Suriname, with documentary evidence.

[102] **Lewes Roberts.** *The Merchants Map of Commerce.* London, 1671. 431 pp.

A geographical description of commerce in the 17th century; also covers commercial interests in America. First published in 1638.

[103] **Charles de Rochefort.** *Le Tableau de L'isle de Tobago, ou de la Nouvelle Oülachre, l'une des l'isles Antilles de l'Amerique.* Leyden, 1665. 144 pp.

History of the Latvian settlement of Tobago and the conflicts with other colonial powers.

[104] **James Rodway.** *Guiana: British, Dutch and French.* London, 1912. 318 pp.

Historical description of the competition among European powers over rule of the Guiana coast.

[105] **James Rodway.** "The Press in British Guiana," *Proceedings of the American Antiquarian Society* (Worcester, MA), 28 (1919): 274–90.

History of the press in British Guiana, including the role of Portuguese Jews.

[106] **James Rodway** and **Thomas Watt**. *Chronological History of the Discovery and Settlement of Guiana, 1493–1668.* Georgetown, British Guiana, 1888. 240 pp.

One of the most detailed histories of Western Guiana, including specifics on the Jewish settlement there.

[107] **J. S. Roos**. "Additional Notes on the History of the Jews of Surinam," *PAJHS* (Waltham), 19 (1910): 177.

Documentary notes on the Jews in Suriname.

[108] **Cecil Roth**. "Jews and the Guianas — an Early Agricultural Settlement in the 17th Century," *The Jewish Chronicle* (London), 2 Dec. 1938.

[109] **Ph. A. Samson**. *Historische Proeve over de Kolonie Suriname.* Paramaribo, 1948. 15 pp.

A historical analysis of the Jewish settlement in Suriname.

[110] **Ph. A. Samson**. "Voorrechten Aan de Joden in Suriname Verleend," *WIG* (Amsterdam), 31 (1949): 139–42.

Analysis of a document on Jewish rights and privileges in Suriname.

[111] **Ph. A. Samson**. "De Kweekschool op de Joden Savanne," *Teroenga* (Paramaribo), 17 (1956): 7–8.

On the school in the Jewish Savanna, Suriname, and impressions of the Jewish Savanna itself by the author, a Jewish writer of Suriname.

[111a] "Secreete Memorie van Consideratie ontrent het Rapport van Essequibo en Demerary" [1790?]. 56 pp. Manuscript in the John Carter Brown Library.

Secret report of a Dutch colonial administrator and his relations with the local population, including Jews.

[112] **Sigmund Seeligmann**. "David Nassy of Surinam & his 'Lettres Politico-Theologico-Morale sur les Juifs'," *PAJHS*, 22 (1914): 25–38.

A Surinamese Jewish leader who lived in Philadelphia writes a study on Jewish rights and reasons for existence as Jews.

[113] S. Kalb Soestadijk. "De Nassi's in Suriname," *De Vrijdagavond* (Amsterdam), 3 (1926): 224, 239–40, 256, 270–71.

Notes on the Nassi family — leaders of the Jews in Suriname during the first 150 years of settlement.

[114] John Gabriel Stedman. *Narrative, of a Five Years' Expedition Against the Revolted Negroes of Surinam, in Guiana, on the Wild Coast of South America, from the year 1772 to 1777, Elucidating the History of that Country.* London, 1796 (reprinted 1971 & 1972). Vol. I, 407 pp.; vol. II, 404 pp.

Narrative by an officer in the Dutch armed forces on the military campaigns in Suriname, in which he discusses meetings with Jewish planters and describes their way of life. [Ed. note: The critical edition (Baltimore & London, 1988; ed. by Richard Price & Sally Price), prepared from the original ms. of 1790, contains significant differences in language.]

[115] John Gabriel Stedman. *Reize naar Surinamen, en door der Binnenste Gedeelten van Guiana.* Amsterdam, 1799 (reprinted 1974). 522 pp.

A translation based on no. 114, above, and a 1798 French translation.

[116] Alphons Summit. "The Jews in Surinam," *The American Hebrew* (New York), 12 Apr. 1940, pp. 44–45.

[116a] C. A. van Sypesteyn. *Beschrijving van Suriname, historisch-, geographisch- en statistisch overzigt.* The Hague, 1854. 296 pp.

A description of Suriname.

[117] Marten D. Teenstra. *De Landbouw in de Kolonie Suriname.* Groningen, 1835. 135 pp.

Account of the Dutch colony of Suriname, including a rare eyewitness description of the Jewish Savanna, its houses, port, and synagogue.

[118] C. L. Temminck Groll, A. R. H. Tjin a Djie, et al. *De Architektuur van Suriname 1667—1930.* Zutphen, 1973. 364 pp.

A comprehensive illustrated book on architecture in Suriname, including plans and drawings of synagogues and Jewish mansions.

[119] Henri Ternaux-Compans. *Notice Historique sur la Guyane Francaise.* Paris, 1843. 192 pp.

The history of the French settlement in what is today French Guiana.

[120] [Not used; see no. 37a.]

[121] **John Womack Vandercook.** "Jungle Jews," *The Menorah Journal* (Concord, New Hampshire) 14:3 (Mar. 1928): 238–46.

Impressions of the Jews living in Suriname.

[122] [Not used; see no. 73a.]

[123] [Not used; see no. 69a.]

[124] [Not used; see no. 69b.]

[125] [Not used; see no. 116a.]

[126] **James Alexander Williamson.** *English Colonies in Guiana and on the Amazon, 1604–1668.* Oxford, 1923. 191 pp.

Historical description of the early settlement of Europeans on the northern coast of South America.

[127] **J. Wolbers.** *Geschiedenis van Suriname.* Amsterdam, 1861. 849 pp.

A detailed history of Suriname in its colonial period.

[128] **Lucien Wolf.** "American Elements in the Resettlement," *TJHSE* (London), 3 (1899): 82–84.

A short article on Jewish settlement in America, including the Guianas.

[129] **Henry Iles Woodcock.** *A History of Tobago.* Ayr: Smith & Grant, 1867. 193 pp.

[130] [Not used; see no. 99a.]

[131] [Not used; see no. 111a.]

[132] **Jacob Zwarts.** "Een Episode uit de Joodsche Kolonisatie van Guyana 1660," *WIG* (Amsterdam), 9 (1927–1928): 519–30.

A description of the Jewish settlement in Pomeroon, Guyana, based on documents in the Amsterdam archives.

II

Netherlands Antilles: Curaçao

[133] **Yaakov Beller.** "הקהילה היהודית העתיקה בקורסאו" ("The Ancient Jewish community in Curaçao"), *Bama'arakha*,1956, pp. 18–19.

Notes on the Jewish community in Curaçao.

[134] **Bernard R. Buddingh'.** *Van Punt en Snoa. Ontstaan en groei van Willemstad, Curaçao vanaf 1634, De Willemstad tussen 1700 en 1732 en de bouwgeschiedenis van de synagoge Mikve Israel-Emanuel 1730–1732.* 's Hertogenbosch, 1994.

[135] **Izak Jesurun Cardozo.** *Three Centuries of Jewish Life in Curaçao.* Willemstad, 1954. 49 pp.

A history of the Jews of Curaçao written by the Chief Haham (Rabbi) in the mid-20th century.

[136*] See no. 18, Cardozo de Bethencourt, "Notes on the Spanish and Portuguese Jews".

A short history of the Jewish settlement in Curaçao.

[137] **G. Herbert Cone.** "The Jews in Curaçao," *PAJHS*, 10 (1902): 141–57.

A review of Jewish history in Curaçao, according to documents in the archives of the State of New York.

[138] **Joseph M. Corcos.** *A Synopsis of the History of the Jews of Curaçao, from the Day of Their Settlement, to the Present Time.* Curaçao, 1897. 48 pp.

History of the Jews of Curaçao by a 19th-century rabbi, with further details on the Jewish settlements in Tucacas, Venezuela, and Newport, Rhode Island.

[139] **John de Pool.** *El Primer chispazo de genio — Bolivar en Curaçao.* Panama, 1935. 71 pp.

Description of Simon Bolivar's stay with the Jewish community in Curaçao.

[140] **John de Pool.** *El primer chispazo de genio (una leyenda historica).* Caracas, 1943. 48 pp.

An imaginary narrative of the meetings between Simon Bolivar and Mordechai Ricardo in British-occupied Curaçao.

[141] **John de Pool.** "Biografia de Dr Mordechai Ricardo," *Mundo Israelita* (Caracas). 21 Apr. 1967.

A short biography of Mordechai Ricardo and the story of his relations with Simon Bolivar.

[142] **Anita de Sola Lazaron.** *De Sola Odyssey: A Thousand and One Years.* Richmond, 1966. 63 pp.

Notes and documents on the de Sola family by one of its descendants.

[143] **David de Sola Pool.** "The Burial Society of Curaçao in 1783," *PAJHS,* 22 (1914): 169–72.

[144*] See no. 36, de Sola Pool, "The Mohelim of Curaçao and Surinam".

[145] **Isaac Emmanuel.** "Jewish Education in Curaçao (1692–1802)," *PAJHS,* 44 (1954–55): 215–36.

On the efforts to maintain a high level of Jewish education in Curaçao.

[146] **Isaac Emmanuel.** *Precious Stones of the Jews of Curaçao.* New York, 1957. 584 pp.

A fascinating work presenting the history of the Jews of Curaçao based on the epitaphs on the gravestones of the island's Jewish cemetery. For a review, see no. 168.

[147] **Isaac Emmanuel.** "El Portugues en la Sinagoga 'Mikve Israel' de Curaçao," *Tesoro de los Judios Sefardies* (Jerusalem), 1959: XXV–XXXI.

On the use of the Portuguese language by the Jews of Curaçao.

[148] **Isaac** and **Suzanne Emmanuel.** *History of the Jews of the Netherlands Antilles.* Cincinnati, 1970. 2 vols., 1165 pp.

FIG. 5. Detail from the tombstone of David Senior, 1749, in Curaçao.

A comprehensive, detailed, and fully documented history of the Jews in Curaçao and neighboring Dutch islands.

[149] P. A. Euwens. "De eerste Jood op Curaçao," *WIG* (Amsterdam), 12 (1930): 360–66.

Study on the identity of the first Jewish settler in Curaçao.

[150] P. A. Euwens. "De Joodsche Synagoge op Curaçao," *WIG* (Amsterdam), 16 (1934): 222–31.

On the construction of the first synagogue in Curaçao.

[151] **Carlos Felice Cardot.** "Algunas acciones de los Holandeses en la region del oriente de Venezuela, primera mitad de siglo XVII," *Boletin de la Academia Nacional de la Historia* (Caracas), 14 (1962): 349–72.

Historical account of 17th-century Dutch efforts at settling the coast of western Venezuela.

[152] **J. H. J. Hamelberg.** *De Nederlanders op de West-Indische Eilanden.* Vol. 1: *De Benedenwindsche Eilanden: Curaçao, Bonaire, Aruba.* Amsterdam, 1901. 215 pp. Vol. 2: *De Bovenwindsche Eilanden: St. Eustatius, Saba, St. Maarten.* Amsterdam, 1903. 59 pp.

A detailed historical book on the Dutch islands of the Caribbean containing original texts pertaining to their history, including the Jewish aspect.

[153*] See no. 52, Hoetink, "The Dutch Caribbean and Its Metropolis".

[154] **Piet Huisman.** *Sephardim: the Spirit That Has Withstood the Times.* Son, The Netherlands, 1986. 96 pp.

A history of the Spanish and Portuguese Jews, in which that of the Jews of Curaçao is prominent.

[155] **Yosef Kaplan.** "The Curaçao and Amsterdam Jewish Communities in the 17th and 18th Centuries," *PAJHS*, 72:2 (Dec. 1982): 193–211.

Description of the relations between the Jewish community in Curaçao and that of Amsterdam.

[156] **Frances P. Karner.** *The Sephardics of Curaçao.* Assen, 1969. 84 pp.

History of the Jewish community of Curaçao.

Netherlands Antilles: Curaçao

[157] **A. J. C. Krafft.** *Historie en Oude families van de Nederlandse Antillen.* The Hague: Martinus Nijhoff, 1951. 448 pp.

A genealogical study of the main families in Curaçao and Aruba, including the Jewish ones.

[158] **Zvi Loker.** "Juan de Ylan, Merchant, Adventurer and Colonial Promoter — New Evidence," *Studia Rosenthaliana* (Amsterdam), 17:1 (1983): 22–31.

Biography of the leader of the first group of Jews to reach Curaçao.

[159] **Antonio J. Maduro.** *Spaanse documenten uit de Jaren 1639 en 1640.* Willemstad, 1961. 114 pp.

Documents on the first years of Jewish life in Curaçao.

[160] **M. L. Maduro.** "A Genealogical Note on the Pimentel, Lopez, Sasportas and Rivera Families," *PAJHS*, 42 (1952–53): 303–309.

[161] **Rene Maduro.** *Our Snoa, 5492–5742 . . . Synagogue Mikve Israel.* Willemstad, 1982. 80 pp.

History of the "Mikve Israel" synagogue, written on its 300th anniversary.

[162] **Simeon J. Maslin.** *Guidebook: The historic synagogue of . . . Congregation Mikve Israel-Emanuel of Curaçao.* Willemstad, 1964. 32 pp.

A Curaçao Chief Rabbi describing the congregation of Portuguese Jews there.

[163] **Simeon J. Maslin.** "1732 and 1982 in Curaçao," *PAJHS* (Waltham), 72:2 (Dec. 1982): 157–64.

Historical notes on the Jews of Curaçao.

[164] **Aaron Peller.** *United Netherlands Portuguese Congregation, Curaçao 1615—1984.* Willemstad, 1982. 30 pp.

History of the Portuguese Jewish congregation in Curaçao, written by its rabbi.

[164a] "Rapport van het Eiland Curaçao" [1791?]. 73 pp. Manuscript in the John Carter Brown Library.

Two Dutch special commissioners report on the state of the island of Curaçao.

[165] **Romulo Rojas Castro.** "Extractos y Comentarios del Almanaque-Guia de Curazao, 1875, Presencia Sefaradi," *Maguen/Escudo* (Caracas), 57 (Oct.-Dec. 1985): 13–18.

Analysis of the Almanac of Curaçao published in 1875, showing the important Jewish presence in all aspects of life in Curaçao.

[166] [Not used; see no. 169a.]

[167] **Gary Schwartz.** *Willemstad, City of Monuments.* The Hague & Amsterdam, 1990. 121 pp.

Pictorial book on the mansions and monuments of Curaçao, including the Jewish ones. Includes articles by C. L. Temminck Groll, et al. Title is superimposed on the word "Curaçao".

[168] **Malcolm H. Stern.** Review of *Precious Stones of Curaçao: Curaçaoan Jewry 1656–1957*, by Isaac Emmanuel. *AJA* (Cincinnati), 2 (1958): 161–64.

See no. 146.

[169] **Rochelle Weinstein.** "Stones of Memory. Revelations from a Cemetery in Curaçao," *AJA* 44:1 (1992): 81–140.

[169a] **Willem Carel Hendrik Friso, Prince of Orange and Nassau.** *Publicacao e provizional reglamento de Sua Alteza o senhor principe de Orange e Nassau &c Consernente a Nacao Judaica Portuguesa em Curaçao.* The Hague: Jacob Scheltus, 1750. 11 pp.

Preliminary version of rules and regulations promulgated by the Dutch Royal house concerning the Portuguese Jews of Curaçao. The Dutch title for this dual-language publication is "Publicatie en provisioneel reglememt, [sic] van Zyne Hoogheid . . . Raakende de Portugeesche Joodsche Natie."

[170] **Willem Carel Hendrik Friso, Prince of Orange and Nassau.** *Reglamento Consernente a Nacao Judaica Portuguesa em Curaçao.* The Hague, 1750. 12 pp.

Rules and regulations promulgated by the Dutch Royal house concerning the Portuguese Jews of Curaçao.

[171] **Yosef Hayim Yerushalmi.** "Between Amsterdam and New Amsterdam. The Place of Curaçao and the Caribbean in Early Modern Jewish History," *PAJHS*, 72:2 (Dec. 1982): 172–92.

The article stresses the importance in Jewish history of the Jewish communities in Curaçao and the West Indies.

Netherlands Antilles: Curaçao

[172] [Not used; see no. 164a.]

III

Netherlands Antilles: St. Eustatius, Aruba, St. Maarten

[173] **Evangeline Walker Andrews**, ed. *Journal of a Lady of Quality*. See no. 193a.

[174] **Mordechai Arbell.** "הקהילה היהודית בסט״ יוסטסיוס" ("The Jewish Community of St. Eustatius"), *Peamim* (Jerusalem), 51 (1992): 124–34.

History of the settlement, life, and destruction of the St. Eustatius Jewish community.

[175] **Yipie Attema.** *St. Eustatius, Historical Gem of the Caribbean.* St. Eustatius, 1978. 8 pp.

Tourist booklet for St. Eustatius which includes the Jewish sites.

[175a] "Debate on Mr. Burke's motion relating to the Seizure and Confiscation of Private Property in the Island of St. Eustatius," in *The Parliamentary History of England from the Earliest Period to the Year 1803*, vol. 22 (Mar. 26, 1781–May 7, 1782). London, 1814. Pp. 218–262.

Motion of Edmund Burke in the British Parliament to censure Admiral Rodney and General Vaughan, on actions against the Jewish population of St. Eustatius and the confiscation of Jewish property there.

[176] **Aron Di Leone Leoni.** "La communita Sefaradite di Recife e Curaçao e i primi insediamenti ebraici nel nuovo mundo," *Rassegna Mensile di Israel*, 51 (1985): 47–81.

The story of the origin of the Jews in Curaçao and Recife — in the author's words, "the first Jewish settlements in the New World."

[177] **Eli N. Evans.** *Judah P. Benjamin — The Jewish Confederate.* New York, 1988. 467 pp.

A biography of the Jewish secretary of state of the Confederacy, born on the island of St. Croix, Virgin Islands, the son of a family of refugees from the island of St. Eustatius.

[178] **Harry A. Ezratty.** "Komemorasion en Statia," *Aki Yerushalayim* (Jerusalem), Anyo 14 (1993): 15–18.

Description of a ceremony commemorating the Portuguese Jews who lived in St. Eustatius and the Jewish sites still standing there.

[179] **Harry A. Ezratty.** "Statia" (San Juan, Puerto Rico, 1993). 10 pp. Manuscript in the possession of M. Arbell.

Description of a visit to the Jewish sites of St. Eustatius in 1993.

[180] **Hester Garrett.** *Gravestone Inscriptions — St. Eustatius.* St. Eustatius, 1976. 66 pp.

A list of gravestone inscriptions, including the legible ones in the Jewish cemetery of St. Eustatius.

[181] **R. Christopher Goodwin.** *Survey of Honen Dalim, St. Eustatius.* Washington, D.C.: U.S. National Museum of Natural History, 1984. 17 pp.

Survey and proposal for reconstruction of the synagogue on St. Eustatius.

[182*] See no. 152, Hamelberg, *De Nederlanders op de West-Indische Eilanden.*

[183] **J. Hartog.** "The Honen Dalim Congregation of St. Eustatius," *AJA* (Cincinnati), 19 (1967): 60–77.

History of the St. Eustatius Jewish congregation.

[184] **J. Hartog.** *History of St. Eustatius.* Aruba, 1976. 173 pp.

A comprehensive history of the island, including its Jewish history.

[185] **J. Hartog.** *The Jews and St. Eustatius.* St. Maarten, 1976. 67 pp.

History of the Jewish community of St. Eustatius.

[186] **George Alexander Kohut.** "Les Juifs dans les Colonies hollandaises," *Revue des Etudes Juives* (Paris), 31 (1895): 294–97.

A historical essay on the Jews in the Dutch colonies, including the Netherlands Antilles.

FIG. 6. Ruins of the synagogue *Honen Dalim* in St. Eustatius, founded in 1739.

[187] **Manfred R. Lehmann.** "Forgotten Jews Who Saved the American Revolution," *Algemeiner Journal* (Miami), 4 March 1994, pp. 3–4.

A precis on the special connection between the Jews of St. Eustatius and the creation of the United States of America.

[188] **Seymour B. Liebman.** "Los Judios de San Eustaquio y la Revolucion Americana," *Herencia Judia* (Bogota), 11 (1976): 19–25.

An article on documentary evidence of the role of St. Eustatius Jews in aiding the American Revolution.

[189] **Seymour B. Liebman.** "Los Judios de San Eustatius y la Revolucion Americana," *Maguen/Escudo* (Caracas), 54 (June–Sept. 1987): 45–48.

On the help given by the St. Eustatius Jews to the American Revolution, leading to the destruction of the Jewish community there.

[190] [Not used; see no. 175a.]

[191] **Serge Plot.** "Les Juifs de Saint-Eustache," *Courier* (Paris), 101 (June 1993): 29–31.

[192] **James Rodway.** *The West Indies and the Spanish Main.* London, 1896. Pp. 238–45.

This history of the West Indies makes special mention of Jewish life in St. Eustatius.

[193] "St. Eustatius," *Massachusetts Spy* (Worcester, Mass.), 28 Apr. 1781, p. 9.

Publication of the petition by the St. Eustatius Jews who had been arrested and had their property confiscated by the British occupying forces.

[193a] **Janet Schaw.** *Journal of a Lady of Quality — Being the Narrative of a Journey from Scotland to the West Indies . . . in the Years 1774 to 1776.* New Haven, 1922. 339 pp.

Narrative by a British woman visiting St. Eustatius in the 18th century, including a description (p. 136–7) of her meeting Jews there. Edited by Evangeline Walker Andrews, in collaboration with Charles McLean Andrews.

[194] **John Singleton.** *A General Description of the West-Indian Islands . . . from Barbados to Saint Croix.* Bridgetown, Barbados, 1767. 159 pp.

A description of the West Indian islands which mentions Jewish life in St. Eustatius and the prosperity of its Jews.

[195] **S. S. Strouse.** "The genesis and the exodus, life and death of Jews on St. Eustatius," *Jewish Digest* (New York), 7 (1962). 21 pp.

A short history of Jews on St. Eustatius through to the community's destruction.

[196] **Samuel S. Strouse.** "Some Aspects of the Early Jewish Community on the Island of St. Eustatius in the Netherlands Antilles" (February, 1962). 10 pp. Manuscript in the American Jewish Archives, Cincinnati.

A study on the formation of the Jewish community in St. Eustatius.

[197] **Edna Vosper.** *Report on the Sir John Vaughan Papers in the William L. Clements Library.* Ann Arbor, Mich., 1929. 37 pp.

Description of the investigation into General Vaughan's activities after his participation in the destruction of the Jewish community of St. Eustatius.

IV

Barbados

[198] **P. Altman.** "Bridgetown Synagogue Restoration Report," *Barbados Jewish News* (Bridgetown), May 1988: 2–3.

Report on the restoration of the old synagogue "Nidhei Israel" by the Barbados Jewish community.

[199] **R. D. Barnett.** "Tombstones in Barbados," *Tesoro de los Judios Sefardies* (Jerusalem), 2 (1959): XLV–XLVI.

Description of the Jewish cemetery in Barbados.

[200] **Hilary Beckles.** A History of Barbados: from Amerindian Settlement to Nation-State. Cambridge, 1990. 224 pp.

[201] **Frederik Jozef Belinfante.** *Geneology of the Belinfante Family.* Gresham, Oregon, 1988. 7 pp.

The diaspora of the Belinfante family in Jamaica, Barbados, Amsterdam, and London.

[202] **Richard Blome.** *A Description of the Island of Jamaica, with the other Isles and Territories in America in which English are Related.* London, 1672. 172 pp.

A detailed description of Jamaica and Barbados everyday life in the second half of the 17th century.

[202a] **Georges-Marie Butel-Dumont.** *Histoire et commerce des Antilles Angloises.* Paris, 1758. 284 pp.

A description of British commercial enterprise in Barbados and Jamaica in which the problem of Jewish rights is discussed.

[203] **Henry J. Cadbury.** "Quakers, Jews and Freedom of Teaching in Barbados 1686," *Bulletin of the Friends Historical Association* (Haverford, Pa.), Autumn 1940: 97–106.

A study on the interreligious relations among the first settlers on Barbados.

[204] **P. F. Campbell.** *An Outline of Barbados History.* Bridgetown: Caribbean Graphics, 1974. Pp. 27–28.

[205*] See no. 18, Cardozo de Bethencourt, "Notes on the Spanish and Portuguese Jews".

Documentary evidence on the Jewish settlers in Barbados.

[206] *Caribbeana. Containing Letters and Dissertations . . . wrote by Several Hands in the West-Indies.* London, 1741. Vol. I, 403 pp.; vol. II, 358 pp.

Essays on general Caribbean history, with special attention to Barbados.

[207] **Eliakim Carmoly.** "La Famille Belinfante," *Revue Orientale* (Brussels), 3 (1843–44): 134–38.

On the Belinfante family, some of whose members were leaders of the Jewish community in Barbados.

[208] **Alfonso Cassuto.** "Items from the Old Minute Book of the Sephardic Congregation of Hamburg. Relating to the Jews of Barbados," *PAJHS*, 32 (1931): 114–15.

Informative items on the relations between the Portuguese Jewish communities of Barbados and Hamburg.

[209] **Edward D. Coleman.** "Bridgetown, Barbados," *PAJHS*, 34 (1937): 275–78.

Cites Wilfred S. Samuel's research on the last days of the Portuguese Jewish community of Bridgetown at the opening of the 20th century.

[210] **N. Darnell Davis.** "Notes on the History of the Jews of Barbados," *PAJHS*, 18 (1909): 129–48.

A well-documented essay on the history of the Barbados Jews.

[211] **N. Darnell Davis.** "Additional Notes on the History of the Jews of Barbados," *PAJHS*, 19 (1910): 173–77.

Additional documents on Barbados Jewish life.

[212] **N. Darnell Davis.** "Notes from wills of the family of Massiah of Barbados," *PAJHS*, 22 (1914): 178–80.

Jewish wills from Barbados provide a window into its Jewish daily life.

FIG. 7. The marble laver at the synagogue *Nidhei Israel* in Bridgetown, Barbados, presently in the Barbados Historical Museum.

[213]   **N. Darnell Davis, Frank Cundall,** and **Albert M. Friedenberg.** "Documents Relating to the History of the Jews in Jamaica and Barbados in the Time of William III," *PAJHS,* 23 (1915): 25–29.

Description of the condition of the Jews in Barbados at the end of the 17th century, and the Jews' petition to King William (1689–94) asking for equal rights.

[214]   **Richard S. Dunn.** "The Barbados Census of 1680: Profile of the Richest Colony in English America," *William and Mary Quarterly.* 3rd. ser., 26:1 (1969): 3–30.

A demographic study on the Barbados population in the late 17th century.

[215]   **P. A. Farrar.** "The Jews in Barbados," *The Journal of the Barbados Museum and Historical Society* (Bridgetown), 9:3 (May 1942): 130–34.

[216]   **Stephen A. Fortune.** *Merchants and Jews: the Struggle for British West Indian Commerce, 1650–1750.* Gainesville, Fla., 1984. 244 pp.

Description of the efforts made by British merchants in Barbados against Jewish commerce.

[217]   **George Frere.** *A Short History of Barbados, from Its First Discovery and Settlement to the end of the year 1767.* London, 1768. 123 pp.

Barbados's colonial history and the tensions involved, its relations with England, and the rule of the Willoughby family.

[218]   **Lee M. Friedman.** "Joshua Montefiore of St. Albans, Vermont," *PAJHS,* 40 (1950–51): 119–34.

The family connection between Joshua Montefiore and the Montefiore family of Barbados.

[219]   **Max Grunwald.** *Portugiesengräber auf deutscher Erde.* Hamburg, 1902. Pp. 105, 107, 120, 150.

Portuguese Jewish graves in Hamburg and their relevance to Barbados.

[220]   **V. T. Harlow.** *A History of Barbados, 1625–1685.* Oxford, 1926. 347 pp.

A detailed history of Barbados and its first years of settlement.

[221] **Samuel Hayne.** *An Abstract of All the Statutes Made concerning Aliens trading in England.* London, 1685. 38 pp.

Included in the abstract are observations trying to prove that the Jews in Barbados break all laws, to the detriment of His Majesty's plantations in America.

[222] **Manfred R. Lehmann.** "Early Relations between American Jews and Eretz Yisrael," *Algemeiner Journal* (Miami), 20 Mar. 1992, pp. 9–10.

On the messengers from the Holy Land to the American continent and Haham Rafael Hayim Carigal in Barbados, and a description of the close relations between the Jews who settled in America and the Holy Land.

[223] **Richard Ligon.** *A True & Exact History of the Island of Barbados.* London, 1657. 122 pp.

A history of the early years of settlement in Barbados.

[224] "The Lucas Manuscript Volumes in the Barbados Public Library," *The Journal of the Barbados Museum and Historical Society* (Bridgetown), 14:1 & 2 (Nov. 1946–Feb. 1947): 70–94.

Section 'The Jews' (pp. 84–94) provides documentary evidence on Jewish life in Barbados.

[225] [Not used; see no. 202a.]

[226] **Vere Langford Oliver.** *Monumental Inscriptions in the Churches and Churchyards of the Island of Barbados.* London, 1915. 223 pp.

A detailed survey of graveyards in Barbados, including the Jewish ones.

[227] **Samuel Oppenheim.** "The Jews in Barbados in 1739 — an Attack upon their Synagogue," *PAJHS*, 22 (1914): 197–98.

On the causes behind the attack against the synagogue "Zemah David" and its destruction in Speightown, Barbados.

[228] **Samuel Oppenheim.** "Extract from an Old Document found amongst the papers in the Cathedral and Parish Church of Barbados," *PAJHS*, 26 (1918): 250–56.

Details of a document describing the special taxes levied on Jews and their commerce. Compiled by Edward S. Daniels and submitted by Samuel Oppenheim.

[229] **Wilfred S. Samuel.** "Will of Rabbi Carigal," *PAJHS*, 31 (1928): 242–43.

Contents of the Hebron Haham Rafael Hayim Carigal's will, demonstrating his strong attachment to the Holy Land.

[230] **Wilfred S. Samuel.** "Review of the Jewish Colonists in Barbados 1680," *TJHSE*, 13 (1932–1935, 1936): 1–112.

One of the best histories of the Jewish community in Barbados, the article also contains statistics, documents, and inscriptions.

[231] [Not used; see no. 209.]

[232] **Sir Robert H. Schomburgk.** *The History of Barbados.* London, 1848. 722 pp.

A highly detailed, well documented history of Barbados, including the efforts towards equality for the Jews under Barbados legislation.

[233] **E. M. Shilstone.** *Monumental Inscriptions in the Burial Ground of the Jewish Synagogue at Bridgetown, Barbados.* Bridgetown, Barbados, 1956, 204 pp.; another edition, [Waltham, Mass.:] American Jewish Historical Society, 1956. 204 pp.

A complete list of inscriptions in the Jewish cemeteries in Bridgetown, including those in Hebrew.

[234] **E. M. Shilstone.** "The Jewish Synagogue," in *Chapters in Barbados History. First Series* (St. Ann's Garrison, Barbados, 1986), pp. 141–52.

The history of the Bridgetown "Nidhei Israel" synagogue and the different stages of rebuilding during the 17th, 18th, and 19th centuries.

[234a] **Ezra Stiles.** *The Event is with the Lord. Correspondence between Ezra Styles and Haham Haim Carigal of Barbados, 1775.* [Cincinnati:] American Jewish Archives, 1976. 6 pp.

Correspondence between Ezra Stiles of Yale University and the Hebron Haham (Rabbi) Carigal in Barbados after their meeting in Newport, Rhode Island. Edited by Stanley F. Chyet.

[235] **Edward Stoute.** "The Jews of Speightown — Barbados," *Advocate Magazine* (Barbados), 1978: 2–3.

Description of the attack on the synagogue "Zemah David" in Speightown and its destruction.

[236] **Lucien Wolf.** "The Family of Gideon Abudiente," in his *Essays in Jewish History*. London: The Jewish Historical Society of England, 1934. Pp. 171–76.

History of the Barbadian Jewish Obediente family and its wandering to the island of Nevis and to London.

V

Jamaica

[237] **Jacob A. P. M. Andrade.** *A Record of the Jews in Jamaica from the English Conquest to the Present Times.* Kingston, 1941. 282 pp.

A monumental historical work describing the life of Jews in Jamaica, their communities all over the island, their synagogues, religious life, and contribution to Jamaica. See also no. 291 for an index to this work.

[238] **Thomas August.** "Jewish Assimilation and the Plural Society in Jamaica," *Social and Economic Studies,* 36:2 (June 1987): 109–22.

An analysis of the position of the Jews in Jamaican society and their struggle for equal rights.

[239] **Thomas August.** Review of *Minorities and Power in a Black Society* by Carol S. Holzberg. *AJA,* 40:1 (1988): 169–73.

[240] **Thomas G. August.** "Family Structure and Jewish Continuity in Jamaica since 1655," *AJA,* 41:1 (1989): 27–44.

Sociological study of Jewish family life in Jamaica.

[241] **Wilma R. Bailey.** "Social control in the Preemancipation Society of Kingston, Jamaica," *Boletin de Estudios Latinoamericanos y del Caribe,* no. 24 (1978): 97–110.

The position of different ethnic groups in Jamaica and their standing vis-a-vis the white society.

[242*] See no. 202, Blome, *A Description of the Island of Jamaica.*

Description of life in Jamaica in the 17th century, including Port Royal before its destruction, life in villages, and Jewish life there.

[243] **Sir Alan Burns.** *History of the British West Indies.* London, 1954. 821 pp.

A well-written historical work which includes the history of Jamaica. Jews in Jamaica are discussed on pp. 446, 513, 625, and 653.

[243a*] See no. 202a, Butel-Dumont, *Histoire et commerce des Antilles Angloises*.

[244] **Concepcion Cabezas Alguacil.** "Un Acercamiento a la obra de Daniel Lopez Laguna, Espejo Fiel de Vidas," *Miscelanea de Estudios Arabes y Hebraicos* (Granada), 37 (1991): 151–62.

On the literary works of the Spanish Jewish writer Daniel Lopez Laguna, including his years in Jamaica.

[245] **Jacob Carciente.** "Dispersion y unidad de la Nacion Judia en el area del Caribe," *Maguen/Escudo* (Caracas), no. 62 (Jan.–Mar. 1987): 8–16.

Publication of a speech made by Dr. Carciente at the opening of "La Nacion" exhibition in Caracas, 1987, in which he describes along general lines, the history of the Jews in the Caribbean, and tells their story.

[246*] See no. 18, Cardozo de Bethencourt, "Notes on the Spanish and Portuguese Jews".

A short description of Jewish settlement in Jamaica (pp. 9–14).

[247] [Not used; see no. 274a.]

[248] **Thomas Coke.** *A History of the West Indies.* Liverpool, 1808. Vol. I, 459 pp. (pp. 216–370); vol. II, 463 pp. (pp. 3–17); vol. III, 541 pp.

A history of the British West Indies, including the history of Jamaica and its Jews.

[249] **G. R. Coulthard.** "The Inscriptions on Jewish Gravestones in Jamaica," *Jamaica Journal* (Kingston), 2 (Mar. 1968): 8–9.

Some inscriptions found in Jewish cemeteries scattered all over the island of Jamaica.

[250] **Frank Cundall.** "Press and Printers of Jamaica Prior to 1820," *Proceedings of the American Antiquarian Society* (Worcester, Mass.), 26:2 (Oct. 18, 1916): 290–412.

History of printing in Jamaica, including the printing of Jewish religious books.

FIG. 8. The decanter given to Moses Delgado in 1831 for helping the Jews of Jamaica to obtain equal rights. The decanter is in the synagogue *Shaare Shalom* in Kingston, Jamaica.

[251]   **Frank Cundall.** "The Taxation of Jews in Jamaica," *PAJHS*, no. 28 (1922): 238–39.

A description of the Jamaican taxation policy under which, until the 20th century, Jews were taxed more than other inhabitants.

[252]   **Frank Cundall.** "The Taxation of the Jews in Jamaica in the 17th Century," *PAJHS*, no. 31 (1928): 243–47.

On the discrimination against Jamaican Jews in taxation during the 17th century.

[253*] See no. 213, N. Darnell Davis, Frank Cundall, and Albert M. Friedenberg, "Documents Relating to the History".

Description of the condition of the Jews in Jamaica and Barbados at the end of the 17th century and the Jews' petition to King William (1689–94) asking for equal rights.

[254]   **Rosemarie DePass Scot.** "Spanish Portuguese Jews in Jamaica, Mid 16th–Mid 17th Centuries," *Jamaica Journal*, 13:1 (1980): 91–100.

[255*] See no. 216, Fortune, *Merchants and Jews. The Struggle for British West Indian Commerce, 1650–1750.*

A richly documented book describing the bitter competition between British and Jewish merchants over commerce in Jamaica and on the American continent.

[256]   **Herbert Friedenwald.** "Material for the History of the Jews in the West Indies," *PAJHS*, 5 (1897): 45–101.

[257]   **Fernando Henriques.** *Jamaica, Land of Wood and Water.* London, 1960.

A passage (on page 23), important for research on the Jewish history of Jamaica, states that Portugallo Colon, Marquis of Jamaica, agreed to allow Jews to settle on the island in 1530 as "New Christians."

[258]   **Capt. Edmund Hickeringill.** *Jamaica Viewed.* London, 1661. 87 pp.

Description of Jamaica in the years following the British occupation in 1655.

[259] **Richard Hill.** *Eight Chapters in the History of Jamaica, from A.D. 1508 to A.D. 1680, Illustrating the Settlement of the Jews on the Island.* Kingston, 1868.

Description of the different waves of Jewish settlement in Jamaica, from the beginning, with Portuguese conversos under Spanish rule, through to Jews under British rule which began in 1655. In the chapter "illustrating the settlement of the Jews" (pp. 4–5), the assumption is that crypto-Jews settled in Jamaica after 1530.

[260] **Carol S. Holzberg.** *Minorities and Power in a Black Society: The Jewish Community of Jamaica.* Lanham, Md., 1987. 259 pp.

Study of interracial relations in Jamaica, featuring the Jewish population. For a review of this work, see no. 240.

[261] **Bernard Hooker.** *United Congregation Shaare Shalom, Kingston.* Kingston: Shaare Shalom, 1980. 8 pp.

Description of the contemporary Jewish congregation in Kingston.

[262] **Samuel** and **Edith Hurwitz.** "The New World Sets an Example for the Old: The Jews of Jamaica and Political Rights, 1661–1831," *PAJHS*, 48 (1958–59): 37–56.

The Jews of Jamaica and their struggle for equal rights.

[263] **Samuel** and **Edith Hurwitz.** *Jamaica, A Historical Portrait.* New York, 1971. 273 pp.

History of Jamaica, including its Jewish history.

[264] *Interesting tracts, relating to the Island of Jamaica, Consisting of Curious State-Papers, Councils of War, Letters, Petitions, Narratives, &c. . . . to the year 1702.* St. Iago de la Vega (Spanish Town), 1800. 300 pp.

A collection of tracts and letters relating to the first years of British rule in Jamaica, in which it is noted that the Portuguese were permitted to stay in Jamaica after the English conquest. A copy is in the John Carter Brown Library.

[265] **Sir Anthony Jenkinson.** "St. Paul's Church Tower in Port Royal" (1964). Manuscript in the American Jewish Archives, Cincinnati, SC5073.

The manuscript describes an English Surveyor's Report of 1688 which mentions the existence of a Jewish synagogue in Port Royal.

[266] **Eugene Johnson.** "The Sephardim of Jamaica," *New Era Magazine* (New York), 3:6 (Nov. 1903): 44–52.

The first settlement of Jews in Jamaica, their origin, and their rights as citizens.

[267] *The Journals of the Assembly of Jamaica.* Jamaica, 1709–1826. Vol. 12 (1808), pp. 30, 46, 47, 67, 82.

A petition by wardens and elders of the Spanish and Portuguese Jews of the city of Kingston to the Assembly of Jamaica for the purpose of legally arranging for the collection of funds for the poor.

[268] **George Fortunatus Judah.** "History of the Jews of Jamaica," *The Daily Telegraph* (Kingston), 25 July 1900 et seq.

[269] **George Fortunatus Judah.** "The Jews' Tribute in Jamaica. Extracted from the Journals of the House of Assembly of Jamaica," *PAJHS*, 18 (1909): 149–77.

Details on the special taxation of the Jews in Jamaica.

[270] **Meir Kayserling.** "The Jews in Jamaica and Daniel Israel Lopez Laguna," *The Jewish Quarterly Review* (London), 12 (Jan. 1900): 708–17.

A well-documented short history of the first Jewish settlements in Jamaica and the Jews' fight for equal rights, as well as the life story of the famous poet of Jamaica Jewry, Daniel Lopez Laguna, including his activity in Jamaica's Jewish community. The article contains good English translations of some of Lopez Laguna's poems.

[271] **Max Kohler.** "Early Jewish Soldiers in London and Jamaica," *PAJHS*, 19 (1910): 179–80.

[272] **Bertram W. Korn.** "The Haham de Cordova of Jamaica," *AJA*, 18:2 (Nov. 1966): 141–54.

An essay on one of the members of the De Cordova family, famous for its religious leaders, newpapermen, and politicians in Jamaica.

[273]   **Manfred Lehmann.** "Pre-Nuptial Agreements in Colonial Days — Their Lessons for Us," *Algemeiner Journal* (Miami), 10 Mar. 1993, pp. B3–B4.

[274]   **Alicia Lindo.** "A Sketch of the Life of David Lindo," *PAJHS*, 23 (1915): 37–41.

[274a] **Marion Clayton Link.** "Exploring the Drowned City of Port Royal," *The National Geographic Magazine*, 117:2 (Feb. 1960): 151–82.

A report by a research team of the National Geographic Society and the Smithsonian Institution which studied and mapped the city of Port Royal, almost completely swallowed by an earthquake. The article's map, prepared by the team, allegedly pinpoints the site of the Jewish synagogue.

[275]   **Zvi Loker.** "An Eighteenth-Century Plan to Invade Jamaica: Isaac Yeshurun Sasportas — French Patriot or Jewish Radical Idealist?" *TJHSE* (London), 28 (1984): 132–44.

Description of an intended French invasion of Jamaica to which a Portuguese Jew was party.

[276]   [Not used; see no. 290a.]

[277]   **Edward Long.** *History of Jamaica.* London: 1774. Vol. I, 626 pp.; vol. II, 502 pp.; vol. III, 420 pp.

A detailed history of the British government in Jamaica.

[278]   **Jacob R. Marcus.** *The Colonial American Jew, 1492–1776.* Detroit: 1970. Pp. 85–211.

The book also covers the relations of Jamaican Jews with North America.

[279]   [Not used; see no. 241a.]

[280]   **Lady Maria Nugent.** *Journal of her Residence in Jamaica from 1801 to 1805.* Kingston, 1966. 331 pp.

Narrative by the wife of the British Governor of Jamaica at the beginning of the 19th century; included are descriptions of aspects of local Jewish life and Jewish military units; mentions an invitation to a Jewish wedding.

[281]   **Samuel Oppenheim.** "Charles II and His Contract with Abraham Israel de Piso and Abraham Cohen for the Working of

a Gold Mine in Jamaica, March 5, 1662–3 and Denization Certificate," *PAJHS*, 19 (1910): 161–67.

Provides text of royal indenture.

[282] "Records of a West Indian Mohel," *PAJHS*, 25 (1917): 114–18.

[283] **Joseph R. Rosenbloom.** "Notes on the Jews' Tribute in Jamaica," *TJHSE* (London), 20 (1959–60): 247–54.

Documents on the special taxation of the Jews in Jamaica.

[284] **Cecil Roth.** "Jews of Jamaica and St Michael," *The Jewish Chronicle* (London), 24 Jan. 1962.

[285] **Benjamin Schlesinger.** "The Jews of Jamaica. A Historical View," *Caribbean Quarterly* (Kingston), 13 (1967): 46–53.

[286] **Henry P. Silverman.** "The Hunt's Bay Jewish Cemetery, Kingston, Jamaica," *PAJHS*, 37 (1947): 327–44.

List and description of the tombstones in one of Jamaica's Jewish cemeteries.

[287] **Henry Phillips Silverman.** *The Tercentenary of the Official Founding of the Jewish Community of Jamaica 1655–1955.* Kingston, 1955. 19 pp.

A short description of the Jewish community in Jamaica. Also titled: *A Panorama of Jamaica Jewry.*

[288] **Henry Phillips Silverman.** *The Seventy-Fifth Anniversary of the Founding of the Synagogue Shaare Shalom, Kingston, Jamaica, 5646–5721.* Kingston, 1960. 27 pp.

A brief history of the main Jewish congregation in Kingston. Also titled: *A Panorama of Jamaica Jewry.*

[289] **Hans Sloane.** *A Voyage to the Islands Madera, Barbados, Nieves, S. Christophers and Jamaica.* London, 1707–1725. Vol. I, 264 pp. plus introduction of 44 pp.; vol. II, 499 pp. plus introduction of 18 pp.

Narrative on the state of life on various islands, including Jamaica.

[290] **Ernest Henriquez de Sousa.** *Pictorial Featuring Some Aspects of Jamaica's Jewry.* Kingston: Congregation Shaare Shalom, 1986. 329 pp.

A pictorial collection presenting all aspects of Jewish life in Jamaica.

[290a] **West India Proprietor.** *A Refutation of various calumnies against the West India Colonies in a series of letters addressed to the editor of the Times and which appeared in that newpaper under the signature of West India proprietor.* London, 1824. 143 pp.

Letters to the editor of the London *Times*, including complaints by the governor of British Honduras against Jamaican Jews.

[291] **Paul F. White.** *Table of contents and biographical Index to Andrade's A Record of the Jews in Jamaica.* Berkeley, Calif., 1964. [33] lvs.

See no. 237 for Andrade's work.

[292] **Dorit Wilson.** "List of Wills in the West Indies Institute, Kingston." 12 pp. Manuscript in the West Indies Institute, now the Institute of Jamaica, Kingston.

Jamaican Jewish wills, useful for research into Jamaican Jewish history and life.

[293] **Philip Wright.** *Jewish Tombstone Inscriptions.* Kingston, 1976.

Inscriptions on some of the old tombstones found in the dispersed Jewish cemeteries in Jamaica.

[294] **Melvin R. Zager.** "Aspects of the Economic, Religious and Social History of the 18th Century Jamaican Jews Derived from Their Wills" (1956). 18 pp. Manuscript (term paper) in the Hebrew Union College Library, Cincinnati.

The wills of Jamaica Jews show various economic, social, and religious aspects of their life.

[295] **David M. Zielonka.** "A Study of the Life of the Jews in Jamaica as Reflected in Their Wills 1692–1798" (1963). 14 pp. Manuscript in the American Jewish Archives, Cincinnati.

An analysis of wills left by Jamaican Jews, which shows different attitudes concerning property, religion, slaves, and family.

VI

The Virgin Islands: St. Thomas and St. Croix; and the Island of Nevis

[296] **Alexander Alland.** "The Jews of the Virgin Islands: a history of the islands and candid biographies of outstanding Jews born there," *The American Hebrew* (New York), 29 Mar. 1940, pp. 12–13; 5 Apr. 1940, pp. 6–7; 26 Apr. 1940, pp. 12–13; 17 May 1940, pp. 4–6, 11–13.

A series of short articles on Jewish life in the Virgin Islands.

[297] **Enid M. Baa.** "The Preservation of the Sephardic Records of the Island of St. Thomas, Virgin Islands," *PAJHS*, 44 (1954–55): 114–19.

Description of the Jewish records in the St. Thomas archives, written by the then director of the archives in Charlotte Amalie.

[298] **Enid M. Baa.** "Sephardic Communities in the Virgin Islands" (1960). 5 pp. Manuscript in the Enid M. Baa Library and Archives, Charlotte Amalie.

A short history of the Jewish communities on St. Thomas and St. Croix.

[299] **Enid M. Baa.** "About the Savan Jewish Cemetery 1750–1836," (1978). 3 pp. Manuscript in the American Jewish Archives, Cincinnati.

The manuscript, written in St. Thomas, lists the names of people buried in the old Jewish cemetery in Charlotte Amalie, St. Thomas, covering about 40% of those interred between 1750 and 1836.

[300] **Frants Ernest Bille.** "The Manner in which Believers in the Mosaic Faith shall be sworn in the future." Manuscript in the American Jewish Archives, Cincinnati, SC-12922. Translated

from Danish original in the Enid M. Baa Library and Archives, *St. Thomas, Book T. T.*, page 139, no. 1, Jan. 13, 1872, pp. 18–21.

Frants Ernest Bille, Commissioner extraordinary and acting governor of the Danish West Indies, signed on January 13, 1872 the ordinances adopted by the Colonial Council of St. Croix, St. Thomas and St. John on April 19, 1864, regulating the manner in which believers in the Mosaic faith shall be sworn in Court. This action repealed the Danish ordinance of May 10, 1842, that was extended to the West Indies. The English text is official, prepared by Gudny M. Pedersen, official translator, and read in Court.

[301]   **Edward Blyden.** *The Jewish Question.* Liverpool, 1898. Pp. 1–20.

A native of St. Thomas fondly describes growing up as a neighbor to the island's Jewish community and hearing the sermons of the Haham Cardozo in the Jewish synagogue.

[302]   **Albert A. Campbell.** "Note on the Jewish Community of St. Thomas, U.S. Virgin Islands," *Jewish Social Studies*, 4:2 (1942): 161–66.

Some historical aspects of Jewish life on St. Thomas.

[303*]   See no. 18, Cardozo de Bethencourt, "Notes on the Spanish and Portuguese Jews".

Short description of Jewish history in the Virgin Islands (pp. 27–38).

[304]   **Leslie Cooper.** *Rededication. Hebrew Congregation, Blessing and Peace and Acts of Piety.* St. Thomas, 1974. 32 pp.

A special booklet devoted to the rededication of the old Jewish synagogue in Charlotte Amalie, St. Thomas.

[305]   **Jack Cramer.** "Two Hemispheres and Centuries of History Buried in the Jewish Cemetery on Nevis," *The St. Kitts-Nevis Observer* (St. Kitts), 9 Dec. 1994, pp. 19–21.

The Jewish history of Nevis as seen by a local researcher.

[306*]   See no. 177, Evans, *Judah P. Benjamin.*

[307]   **Harry A. Ezratty.** "Old Sephardic Cemetery Reconsecrated in Nevis," *The American Sephardi* (New York), 5 (1971): 132–5.

The reconsecration of the old Jewish cemetery in Nevis.

[308]   **Lee M. Friedman.** "Wills of Early Settlers in New York," *PAJHS*, 23 (1915): 147–61.

This list of wills contains several by Jewish natives of Nevis residing in New York.

[309]   **Lee M. Friedman.** "Gabriel Milan, the Jewish Governor of St. Thomas," *PAJHS*, 28 (1922): 213–21.

On the years of rule of the first Jewish governor of St. Thomas under the Danes, and about their execution of him.

[310]   **Joyce Gordon.** *Nevis, Queen of the Caribees.* London, 1985. 88 pp.

History of Nevis and notes on the Jewish community there.

[311]   [Not used; see no. 317a.]

[312]   **Bernard Heller.** "Epitaphs in the Jewish Cemetery at Christianstad [sic], St. Croix" (1958). 1 p. Manuscript in the possession of M. Arbell.

A list of Jewish tombstones located on St. Croix.

[313]   **Lincoln W. Higgie.** *The Colonial Coinage of the U.S. Virgin Islands.* Racine, Wisc., 1962, 61 pp.

Story and description of tokens specially coined by Jewish commercial houses in St. Thomas.

[314]   **Vincent K. Hubbard.** "Synagogue Rediscovered," Nevis Historical and Conservation Society *Newsletter* (Charlestown, Nevis), Nov. 1991: 1–3.

A theory offered following excavations on Nevis, concerning the supposed site of the synagogue.

[315]   **Leon Hühner.** "David L. Yulee, Florida's First Senator," *PAJHS*, 25 (1917): 1–29.

Biographical article on Yulee, originally from St. Thomas, who was the first Jew in the U.S. Senate as well as Florida's first senator.

[316]   **Max Kohler.** "Judah P. Benjamin — statesman and jurist," *PAJHS*, 12 (1904): 63–85.

Biographical sketch of the secretary of state of the Confederacy, a Jew from St. Croix.

[317] **Bertram W. Korn.** "Judah P. Benjamin as a Jew," *PAJHS*, 38 (1948–49): 153–72.

On the Confederacy's Jewish secretary of state, a native of St. Croix.

[317a] **Frederik Krarup.** "Gabriel Milan og somme af hans samtid," *Personalhistorisk Tidsskrift* (Copenhagen), series 3, vol. 2 (1893): 102–130, vol. 3 (1894): 1–51.

Biography of Gabriel Milan, Jewish governor of St. Thomas under the Danes, who was ultimately executed by the Danish authorities. Pt. 1 treats his earlier career; pt. 2 his governorship of St. Thomas and career thereafter.

[318] **Jens Larsen.** *Virgin Islands Story.* Philadelphia, 1950. 250 pp.

History of the Virgin Islands, including the aspect of Jewish settlement there.

[319] **Florence Lewisohn,** "Alexander Hamilton's West Indian Boyhood," in her *What So Proudly We Hail: The Danish West Indies and the American Revolution* (St. Thomas: American Revolution Bicentennial Commission of the U.S. Virgin Islands, 1975), pp. 17–29.

Alexander Hamilton's boyhood was intimately connected with the Jewish community of Nevis.

[320] **Jul. Margolinsky.** "298 Epitaphs from the Jewish Cemetery in St. Thomas" (Copenhagen: 1952). 34 pp. Manuscript in the possession of M. Arbell.

Jewish inscriptions in the old Jewish cemetery on St. Thomas; the Hebrew inscriptions are not listed.

[321] **Hester Marsden-Smedley.** "The Jews of Nevis," *The Jewish Chronicle* (London), 15 Aug. 1969.

[322] **M. N. Nathan, E. C. Da Costa,** and **I. H. Osorio.** *Code of Laws for the Government of the Israelite Congregation in the Island of St. Thomas.* St. Thomas, 1848. 24 pp.

[323] **Vere Langford Oliver.** "The Jewish Cemetery at Charlestown, Nevis" (Nov. 1923). Manuscript in the possession of the Jewish Historical Society of England.

Several Jewish epitaphs found in the Jewish cemetery on Nevis.

[324] **Karen Fog Olwig.** *Global Culture, Island Identity — Continuity and Change in the Afro-Caribbean Community of Nevis.* Chur, Switzerland, 1993. 239 pp.

In this book describing the life of slaves and black inhabitants of Nevis is a rare description of the Sunday market of Nevis where slaves and Jews traded.

[325] **Isidor Paiewonsky.** *Jewish Historical Development in the Virgin Islands, 1665–1959.* St. Thomas, 1959. 25 pp.

A short history of the Jews of the Virgin Islands.

[326] **Isidor Paiewonsky.** "Camille Pissarro, St. Thomas," *Daily News* (Charlotte Amalie, St. Thomas), 3 Feb. 1975, 10 Feb. 1975, 23 May 1977.

Biographical sketch on the painter Camille Pissarro and his family, French-Portuguese Jews residing in St. Thomas.

[327] **Richard Pares.** *A West-India Fortune.* London, 1950. 374 pp.

The story of a British family in Nevis, with vivid description of life and commerce on the island.

[328] **David Philipson.** "An Early Confirmation Certificate from the Island of St. Thomas, Danish West Indies," *PAJHS*, 23 (1915): 180–82.

The text of an 1864 certificate confirming membership in the Jewish congregation of St. Thomas, and comments on it.

[329] *Pissarro.* Paris: Editions de la Reunion des Musees Nationaux, Ministere de la Culture, 1981. 262 pp.

Exhibition catalog, with biographical notes on the Pissarro family of St. Thomas and on Camille Pissarro's first paintings there.

[330] **Stanley T. Relkin** and **Monty R. Abrams.** *A Short History of the Hebrew Congregation of St. Thomas.* St. Thomas: The Hebrew Congregation of St. Thomas, 1983. 32 pp.

Description of the congregation in St. Thomas, prepared by its religious leaders.

[331] **Jacob Robles.** "St. Thomas Burials 1792–1802" (1970). 3 pp. Manuscript in the possession of M. Arbell.

A list of burials and their dates.

[332] **Jacob Robles.** "Names on Stones in Savan Cemetery, Charlotte Amalie, St. Thomas, So Far Located" (1972). 5 pp. Manuscript in the possession of M. Arbell.

A list of names of people buried in the oldest Jewish cemetery in St. Thomas.

[333] **Jacob Robles.** "St. Thomas Confirmations 1843–1934" (1972). 5 pp. Manuscript in the possession of M. Arbell.

Confirmation lists providing also the names of fathers and mothers; very useful for genealogical study.

[334] **Nathan Schachner.** *Alexander Hamilton.* New York: 1961. 488 pp.

Alexander Hamilton's childhood in the West Indies and his links to the Hebrew communities in St. Thomas and Nevis.

[335] **Malcolm H. Stern.** "Some Notes on the Jews of Nevis," *AJA*, 10:2 (Oct. 1958): 151–59.

Documents on the little-known history of the Jews of Nevis.

[336] **Malcolm H. Stern.** "A Successful Caribbean Restoration, The Nevis Story," *AJHQ* (Waltham), 16 (1972): 19–32.

On the restoration of the old Jewish cemetery in Nevis.

[337] **Waldemar C. Westergaard.** *The Danish West Indies Under Company Rule (1671–1754) with a Supplementary Chapter, 1755–1917.* New York: 1917. 359 pp.

History of the Danish West Indies, including its Jewish communities.

[338] **Kurt Wilhelm.** "Jewish Epitaphs in the West Indies, St. Thomas," *Tesoro de los Judios Sefardies* (Jerusalem), 2 (1959): XLIV–XLV.

Some of the important inscriptions in the old Jewish cemetery in St. Thomas.

[339*] See no. 236, Wolf, "The Family of Gideon Abudiente".

VII

Colombia and Venezuela

[340] **Miguel Acosta Saignes.** *Historia de los Portugueses en Venezuela.* Caracas, 1977. Pp. 21–23.

Notes on the Portuguese conversos in Venezuela.

[341] **Raul Agudo Freites.** *Elias David Curiel, el viento y la peninsula.* Caracas, 1977.

Biography of Elias David Curiel, a writer and poet of Coro, Venezuela.

[342] **Isidoro Aizenberg.** "Judios en la Caracas del 1800," *Menora* (Caracas), Ano 10, no. 150 (Aug.-Sept. 1971).

History of the Portuguese Jewish community in Caracas, written by the rabbi of the city.

[343] **Isidoro Aizenberg.** "Venezuela y los Judios Venezuelanos," *El Universal* (Caracas), Oct. 1971.

Notes on the history of Venezuelan Jewry.

[344] **Isidoro Aizenberg.** "Dos Commerciantes Judios de la Epoca Colonial," *Boletin Historico* (Caracas: Fondacion Boulton), 29 (May 1972): 271–83.

A study of the case of the two Jewish merchants of Curaçao, David Morales and Joseph Obediente, at the beginning of the 19th century, in the context of the commerce between the Dutch and the Spanish colonies.

[345] **Isidoro Aizenberg.** "Die or Leave: An Anti-Jewish Riot in Nineteenth Century Venezuela," *AJH*, 69 (1980): 478–87.

Description of anti-Jewish riots in Coro, Venezuela, in the 19th century.

[346] **Isidoro Aizenberg.** "The 1855 Expulsion of the Curaçaoan Jews from Coro," *AJH*, 72 (1982–83): 495–507.

On anti-Semitic riots in Coro, Venezuela, which led to the expulsion of the Jews.

[347] **Celestino Andres Arauz Monfante.** *El Contrabando Holandes en el Caribe, Durante la Primera Mitad de Siglo XVIII.* Caracas, 1984. Vol. I, 352 pp.; vol. II.

History of the Dutch activities on the Venezuelan coast at the end of the 17th and the beginning of the 18th centuries. The book contains a rare description of the Jewish settlement of Tucacas, settled by Jews from Curaçao at the end of the 18th century.

[348] **Mordehay Arbell.** "Dona Sara de Coro, Venezuela," *Aki Yerushalayim* (Jerusalem), 42 (1990): 16–18.

An interview with the last Portuguese Jewess in Coro, Venezuela.

[349] **Mordehay Arbell.** "Mordehay Ricardo en Timbro," *Aki Yerushalayim* (Jerusalem), 42 (1990): 30–31.

The role of Curaçao's Mordechai Ricardo in the independence of the northern part of South America.

[350] **Dino Manco Bermudez** and **Jose Watnik Baron.** *Nuestras Gentes. Primera Generacion.* Barranquilla, Colombia, 1994. 187 pp.

A compilation of historical facts and documents on the history of the Jews in Barranquilla, Colombia, including information on the first Jewish settlers, who came from Curaçao, and the first publication of a list of graves in the old Sephardi cemetery.

[351] **Jacob Carciente.** "Los Judios de Barcelona (Venezuela)," *Maguen/Escudo* (Caracas), 15 (Aug. 1971): 2–8.

History of the settlement of Portuguese Jews in Barcelona, Venezuela, who were later joined by Jews from Morocco.

[352] **Jacob Carciente.** "Centenario de Nacimiento del Poeta Elias David Curiel," *Maguen/Escudo* (Caracas), 15 (Aug. 1971): 16–17.

Special article describing the work of the most famous Jewish poet of Venezuela, Elias David Curiel, on the 100th anniversary of his birth.

[353] **Jacob Carciente.** *La Comunidad Judia de Venezuela 1610–1990.* Caracas, 1991. 247 pp. (Issued as part of series: Biblioteca Popular Sefardi.)

FIG. 9. The Spanish-Portuguese Jewish cemetery in Barranquilla, Colombia.

FIG. 10. The Spanish-Portuguese Jewish cemetery in Coro, Venezuela, which was declared a Venezuelan national monument in 1970.

History of the Jewish community in Venezuela starting from Spanish colonial times.

[354*] See no. 138, Corcos, *A Synopsis of the History of the Jews of Curaçao*.

Description of the settlement of Curaçao Jews in Tucacas, Venezuela, at the end of the 17th century.

[355] **Itic Croitoru Rotbaum.** *De Sefarad al Neosefardismo — contribucion a la historia de Colombia*. Bogota, 1967. 431 pp.

A rare description of the Portuguese Jews in Barranquilla, Colombia. A second volume published in 1971 (*Documentos coloniales*) contains vital documents of the Inquisition.

[356] **Sonia Delgado.** *De Curazao a Coro, la odisea de los Judios en Venezuela*. Caracas: Elite, 1979. 5 pp.

Notes on the settlement of Curaçao Jews in Coro, Venezuela.

[357*] See no. 139, de Pool, *El primer chispazo de genio*.

[358] **Irma de Sola-Ricardo.** "Juan de Sola, procer de la Independencia y actor de Carabobo," *Boletin Historico* (Caracas), 31 (Jan. 1973): 43–59.

On the life of the Portuguese Jewish general Juan de Sola, fighter for Venezuelan independence from Spain.

[359] **Isaac S. Emmanuel.** *The Jews of Coro, Venezuela*. Cincinnati: American Jewish Archives, 1973. 63 pp.

A comprehensive history of and documentation on Jewish life in Coro, Venezuela, published posthumously.

[360*] See no. 151, Felice Cardot, "Algunas acciones de los Holandeses en la region del Oriente de Venezuela, Primera mitad de siglo XVII".

A history of the Dutch activities off the Venezuelan coast, in which Curaçao, Tucacas, and Pomeroon Jews were involved.

[361] **Jose Rafael Fortique.** *Los Motines Anti-Judios de Coro*. Maracaibo, 1973.

On the anti-Jewish riots in Coro, Venezuela.

[362] **Jose Rafael Fortique.** "Los sucesos de 1831 contra los judios de Coro," *Boletin de la Academia Nacional de la Historia* (Caracas), July-Sept. 1973: 441–45

An article addresssing the anti-Semitic wave and persecution against the Jews of Coro, newly arrived from Curaçao, and the attempts of the authorities to secure the life of the Jews in Coro.

[363] **Juan Friede, ed.** *Gonzalo Jimenez de Quesada a travez de documentos historicos.* Bogota, 1960. 398 pp.

The story of the life of Jimenez de Quesada, founder of Bogota, allegedly of Jewish origin.

[364] **Emil Levy Maduro.** *Esbozo historico novelizado, y versos hechos por Emil L[evy]. Maduro . . . para ofrendar a los manes del culminante general Pedro Leon Torres en su primer centenario del ano 1888.* Barquisimeto, 1888. 27 pp.

Patriotic poems of a Venezuelan Jewish poet.

[365] **Juvenal Lopez Ruiz.** "El Universo Poetico de Elias David Curiel," *Maguen/Escudo* (Caracas), 63 (Apr.–June 1987): 12–23.

An article on the poetry of the Venezuelan Jewish poet Elias David Curiel.

[366] **Daniel Mesa Bernal.** "Los judios en la epoca colonial," *Boletin de Historia y Antiguedades* (Bogota), 73 (1986): 381–99.

An attempt to present the history of crypto-Jews according to the trials of the Cartagena Inquisition, and the story of the Portuguese Jewish settlement in Barranquilla.

[367] **Juan Angel Mogollon.** "El Poeta Elias David Curiel, 1871–1924," *Tesoro de los Judios Sefardies* (Jerusalem), 10 (1968): LXIII–LXVII.

Notes on the Venezuelan Jewish poet, Elias David Curiel.

[368] **Isaac Molho.** "Escritores Sefardies en Venezuela," *Tesoro de los Judios Sefardies* (Jerusalem), 7 (1964): 103–105.

On Venezuelan Jewish writers.

[369] **Mario Nassi.** "La independencia de Venezuela y los judios," *Sefardica* (Buenos Aires), no. 5 (May 1986): 81–91.

On the Jewish participation in the War of Independence of the northern part of South America, and the aid the Jews of Curaçao gave to Bolivar and his army for the liberation of Venezuela.

[370] **Ambrosio Perera.** "Familia Herrera," in his *Historial Genealogico de familias Carorenas.* 2nd ed. (Caracas, 1967), vol. 1, pp. 266–73.

The history of the Jewish family Herrera of Carora, Venezuela.

[371] **Jose Felix Rivero.** "Dr. S. de Jongh Ricardo," *Paginas Hebreas* (Caracas), 30 (1957): 3.

Newspaper editorial written upon the death of one of the most prominent Portuguese Jewish leaders in Venezuela.

[372] **Jose Felix Rivero.** "Coro: 450 Anos de 'Buenaventura de la Luz'," *El Mundo* (Caracas), 26 May 1977, p. 3.

History of the city of Coro, Venezuela.

[373] **Cecilio Zubillaga Perera.** "Homenaje a Don Jacobo Jose Curiel en el centro Lara," *El Diario* (Caracas), 21 Jan. 1946.

Historical article on the Curiel family of Coro and Carora in Venezuela.

VIII

Panama, El Salvador, Costa Rica, Belize

[374] **Pierre Ainbinder.** "Report on Journey to Belize City, Belize — Visit to the Jewish Burial Ground," (Montreal, 1988). 30 pp. Manuscript located with the Commonwealth Jewish Council, London.

Description of the current state of the old Jewish cemetery near Belize City.

[375] **Nadhji Arjona.** *Bob Eisenman Brandon, el Forjador de un Sueno.* Panama: private publication, 1975. 142 pp.

Biography of Bob Eisenman Brandon, one of the prominent Portuguese Jews of Panama.

[376] **Nadhji Arjona.** "Raices Centenares del Pueblo Hebreo en la Republica de Panama," *Revista de Estrella de Panama,* 1 (Oct. 1980): 13–15.

On the Portuguese Jews of Panama and their roots in the American continent.

[377] **Nadhji Arjona.** *La familia Fidanque: cien anos en Panama... 1885... 1985 / The Fidanque Family: Centennial Anniversary in Panama.* Panama, 1986. 108 pp.

The Panamanian history of the Fidanque family, originally from Altona, Hamburg, Curaçao, and St. Thomas.

[378] *La Comunidad Hebrea de Panama.* Panama: B'nai B'rith, 1961. 22 pp.

Description of the Jewish community of Panama.

[379] **Hector de Lima Jesurun.** *La Comunidad Judia de Panama.* Panama, 1977. 24 pp.

History of the Jewish community in Panama.

[380] E. Alvin Fidanque. "Jews and Panama," *The American Sephardi* (New York), 4 (1970): 37-49.

Historical notes on Spanish-Portuguese Jews in Panama.

[381] E. Alvin Fidanque. *Jews and Panama*. [New York?] 1970. 24 p.

History of the settlement of Jews in Panama. Part of this monograph originally appeared as no. 380.

[382] E. Alvin Fidanque, et al. *Kol Shearith Israel — Cien Anos de Vida Judia en Panama 1876–1976 / Kol Shearith Israel — A Hundred Years of Jewish Life in Panama*. Panama, 1977. 487 pp.

History of the Spanish-Portuguese Jewish congregation "Kol Shearith Israel" in Panama. Spanish and English text in facing columns.

[383] Emma Fidanque Levy. "The Fidanques: Symbols of the Continuity of the Sephardic Tradition in America," *AJA* (Cincinnati), 44:1 (1992): 179–208.

The story of the Fidanque family.

[384] Emma Fidanque Levy. *Fidelity, Faith, Freedom: the Fidanques in the Western Hemisphere*. New York, 1993. 34 pp.

History of the Fidanque family which moved from Altona, Hamburg, Curaçao, and St. Thomas to settle in Panama.

[385] Enrique Jaramillo Levi. "La Saga de la Familia Osorio," *Revista Nacional de Cultura* (Panama), Apr. 1992: 65–75.

The history of the Osorio family in Panama.

[386] Maria Leistenschneider. "Presidente Juan Lindo," in her *Gobernantes de El Salvador* (San Salvador, 1980), pp. 58–61.

Among the biographies of the presidents of El Salvador is that of Juan Lindo, president of El Salvador and Honduras, who was of Jewish origin.

[387] "Max Delvalle Henriques, hijo afectuoso de Panama — 1911–1979," *Boletin B'nai B'rith* (Panama), 1980: 31–32.

Brief article on Max Delvalle, Portuguese-Jewish president of Panama.

[388] Joseph Melamed. *1976, Centenario Kol Shearith Israel*. Panama: Bibliographica Ingmar, 1976. 44 pp.

A survey of 100 years of existence of the Spanish-Portuguese congregation of Panama, written by its rabbi.

[389] **Alberto Osorio Osorio.** *Historia de la Ciudad de David.* David, Panama, 1974. 429 pp.

History of the city of David in Panama, founded by the converso Juan Lopez Sequera.

[390] **Alberto Osorio Osorio.** *Judaismo e Inquisicion en Panama Colonial.* Panama, 1980. 245 pp.

History of the secret Jewish life in Panama under Spanish rule.

[391] **Alberto Osorio Osorio.** "La dispersion Crypto-Judia en Panama siglos XVI y XVII," *Sefardica* (Buenos Aires), 7 (1989): 77–92.

Notes on the secret Jewish life in Panama under Spanish rule.

[392] **Albert Osorio Osorio.** *Los Osorios Sefardies, Rutas y Legado.* Panama: private publication, 1991. 317 pp.

History of the Osorio family from Curaçao to St. Thomas to their settlement in Panama.

[393] **Rosita Kalina de Pisk.** "Sefaraditas en Costa Rica antes y despues de siglo XIX," *Maguen/Escudo* (Caracas), 1982: 34–47.

Notes on the Spanish-Portuguese Jewish families in Costa Rica.

[394] **H. P. Salomon.** "The Fidanques, Hidalgos of Faith," *The American Sephardi* (New York), 4:1–2 (1970): 15–36.

History of the Fidanque family.

[395] **Jacobo Schifter.** *El Judio en Costa Rica.* San Jose, Costa Rica: Editorial Universidad Estatal, 1979. 385 pp.

History of the Jews in Costa Rica.

[396] *Special Hymns of Temple Kahal Kados Yangakob.* Colon: Imp. Atlantida, 1961. 13 pp.

Book of prayers of the Spanish-Portuguese congregation in the city of Colon, Panama.

IX

Dominican Republic

[397] **Mordechai Arbell.** "Historia de la familia Lopez-Penha 1660–1924," in Alfonso Lockward, ed., *Presencia Judia in Santo Domingo* (Santo Domingo, 1994), pp. 123–42.

Story of the Lopez-Penha family, based on a family manuscript, which followed a route of Spain-Portugal-Izmir-Amsterdam-Curaçao-Barranquilla until finally settling in Santo Domingo.

[398] **Carlos Esteban Deive,** "Los Judios en Santo Domingo y America durante el siglo XVI," in Alfonso Lockward, ed., *Presencia Judia in Santo Domingo* (Santo Domingo, 1994), pp. 175–92.

History of the first Jews in the Dominican Republic.

[399] **Enrique de Marchena Dujarric.** "Presencia hebrea en la Republica Dominicana," in Alfonso Lockward, ed., *Presencia Judia in Santo Domingo* (Santo Domingo, 1994), pp. 83–102.

The story of Jewish life in the Dominican Republic.

[400] **H. Hoetink.** *El Pueblo Dominicano, 1850–1900, Apuntes para su sociologica historica.* Santiago de los Caballeros, 1971. 351 pp.

The special role of the Jews in the Dominican Republic, and their integration into general society.

[401] **Hyman J. Kisch.** "Los memorables sefaraditas de la Republica Dominicana," *Conservative Judaism* (New York), 28:2 (1974): 16.

Notes on the prominent Spanish-Portuguese families in the Dominican Republic.

[402] **Alfonso Lockward.** "Presencia Judia en Santo Domingo," in Alfonso Lockward, ed., *Presencia Judia in Santo Domingo* (Santo Domingo, 1994), pp. 13–46.

On the Jewish population in Santo Domingo.

[403] **Alfonso Lockward,** ed. *Presencia Judia en Santo Domingo.* Santo Domingo, 1994. 231 pp.

A collection of articles on the history of the Jews in the Dominican Republic, including the topic of the first Portuguese Jews to settle the island, initially as conversos and then as Jews, in the 15th–18th centuries.

[404] **Enrique Ucko.** *La fusion de los Sefardies con los Dominicanos.* Ciudad Trujillo [Santo Domingo],1944. 34 pp.

Description of the relations between the Spanish-Portuguese Jews and the Dominicans.

X

Haiti, Martinique, Guadeloupe

[405] **Mordechai Arbell.** "La Istoria de los Sefardis en las Islas de Martinique, Guadeloupe," *Aki Yerushalayim*, no. 49, Anyo 15 (1994): 20–21.

A short account of Jews in Martinique and Guadeloupe, from the arrival of the first from Brazil in 1654 until their expulsion by the 'Black Code', 1685.

[406] **Archives Nationales, Paris.** "List of Properties Situated in Saint Domingue, having belonged to the Mendes France family." 7 pp. Manuscript in the American Jewish Archives, Cincinnati.

A detailed listing by an anonymous compiler, of material in different French archives on the properties of the Mendes France family in Haiti.

[407] [Not used; see no. 415a.]

[408] [Not used; see no. 421a.]

[409*] See no. 11, Biet, *Voyage de la France equinoxiale en l'isle de Cayenne entrepris par les Francois en l'annee M.DC.LII.*

[410] **Philip P. Boucher.** *Les Nouvelles Frances — France in America, 1500–1815, An Imperial Perspective.* Providence, R.I.: John Carter Brown Library, 1989. 122 pp.

An exhibition catalog with comments on the French colonial activities on the American continent.

[411] **Edner Brutus.** *Revolution dans Saint Domingue.* Brussels, 1968. 406 pp.

History of Haiti under French colonial rule.

[412] **Abraham Cahen.** "Les Juifs dans les colonies francaises au XVIII siecle," *Revue des Etudes Juives* (Paris), 4 (1882): 127–45, 238–72; pieces supplementaires, 5 (1882): 68–92.

Jewish life in Martinique, Guadeloupe, and Haiti before the Jews' expulsion in 1685 and thereafter.

[413] **Abraham Cahen.** "Les Juifs de la Martinique au XVII siecle," *Revue des Etudes Juives* (Paris), 31 (1895): 92–121.

Jewish life in Martinique prior to the expulsion of the Jews in 1685.

[414*] See no. 18, Cardozo de Bethencourt, "Notes on the Spanish and Portuguese Jews".

Notes on Jews in the French colonies (pp. 19–20).

[415] **Jean Cavignac.** *Dictionnaire du Judaisme Bordelais aux XVIIIe et XIXe siecles. Biographies, Genealogies, Professions, Institutions.* Bordeaux, 1987. 305 pp.

The dictionary indicates the close relations of Bordeaux Jews to Jews in Haiti, Martinique, and Guadeloupe.

[415a*] See no. 20a, Clodore, *Relation de ce qui s'est passe dans les Isles et Terre Ferme de l'Amerique, pendant la derniere Guerre avec l'Angleterre et depuis.*

[416*] See no. 26, Crouse, *The French Struggle.*

History of the French attempts to gain rule in the West Indies.

[417] **Nellis Crouse.** *French Pioneers in the West Indies 1624–1664.* New York, 1940. 294 pp.

History of the French settlements in the Caribbean.

[417a*] See no. 37a, Dutertre, *Histoire Generale des Antilles.*

[418] **Isaac Emmanuel.** "Les Juifs de la Martinique et leurs coreligionnaires d'Amsterdam au XVIIe Siecle," *Revue des Etudes Juives* (Paris), 123 (1964): 511–16.

On Jewish life in Martinique in the 17th century.

[419] **Heinrich Graetz.** "Die Familie Gradis," *MGWJ* (Dresden), 24 (1875): 447–59; 25 (1876): 78–85.

Articles on the Gradis family, the most prominent Jewish family in the French Caribbean.

[420] **William Hodges.** *Les Juifs au Cap — evidence d'une communaute juive au Cap Francois.* Limbe, Haiti: Musee de Guahaba, 1985. 11 pp.

Details on the discovery of an old Jewish cemetery in Cap Haitien, Haiti.

[421] **Joseph Janin.** *La Religion aux colonies francaises sous l'Ancien Regime.* Paris, 1942. 232 pp.

A study of the complicated religious life in the French colonies.

[421a*] See no. 61a, La Barre, *Description de la France Equinoctiale cy devant appelee Guyanne et par les Espagnoles "El Dorado".*

[422*] See 62, Labat, *Nouveau Voyage.*

[423] **Jean Baptiste Labat.** *Nuevo Viaje a las Islas de la America.* San Juan, 1984. 279 pp.

Spanish translation of the main parts of Labat's *Nouveau Voyage aux Isles de l'Amerique* (see no. 62).

[424] **Zvi Loker.** "Lopez de Paz 'medecin du roi' a Saint Domingue," *Revue d'histoire de la Medecine Hebraique* (Paris), 119 (1976): 53–55.

Biography of a famous Jewish physician in Haiti.

[425] **Zvi Loker.** "Une famille juive au cap: Membres de la famille Depas a St.-Domingue," *Conjonction: Revue Franco-Haitienne* (Port-au-Prince), 133 (1977): 126–31.

Study on the Spanish-Portuguese family Depas of Haiti.

[426] **Zvi Loker.** "Toponymies juives en Haiti," *Conjonction: Revue Franco-Haitienne* (Port-au-Prince), 135 (1977): 89–98.

A study of personal and place names of Jewish origin in Haiti.

[427] **Zvi Loker.** "Un cimetiere juif au Cap Haitien," *Revue des Etudes Juives* (Paris), 136 (1977): 425–27.

Notes on the old Jewish cemetery in Cap Haitien.

[428] **Zvi Loker.** "Un Juif portugais: fondateur de Moron?" *Conjonction: Revue Franco-Haitienne* (Port-au-Prince), 139 (1978): 85–91.

About the Henriques Moron family of Haiti, founders of the village of Moron.

[429]   **Zvi Loker.** "Simon Isaac Henriquez Moron — homme d'affaires de Grand'Anse," *Revue de la Societe Haitienne d'Histoire* (Port-au-Prince), no. 125 (1979): 56–69.

About the Spanish-Portuguese family of Henriques Moron in Haiti.

[430]   **Zvi Loker.** "Jews in the Grand'Anse Colony of Saint Dominique," *AJA*, 34:1 (1982): 89–97.

On the settlement of Jews in Haiti.

[431]   **Zvi Loker.** "Inventaire des Biens d'Isaac Henriquez Moron — Un Document Inedit de la Grand'Anse, Saint-Domingue," *Conjonction: Revue Franco-Haitienne* (Port-au-Prince), 152 (1982): 5–11.

Documentary evidence on the plantation of the Portuguese Jew Isaac Henriquez Moron, which is now the township of Moron in Haiti.

[432]   **Zvi Loker.** "Were there Jewish Communities in Saint Domingue (Haiti)?" *Jewish Social Studies* (New York), 45:2 (1983): 135–46.

A study on the Jews of Haiti.

[433]   **Zvi Loker.** "The Expulsion of the Jews from Martinique 1684," in *Misgav Yerushalayim* (1994), pp. 328–31.

Notes on Jewish life in Martinique until the expulsion of the Jews in 1685.

[434]   **Louis XIV, Roi de France et Navarre.** *Le Code Noir ou Edit du Roy — servant de Reglement touchant la Police des Isles de l'Amerique Francaise.* Versailles, 1685. 15 pp.

The text of the 'Black Code' issued by Louis XIV ordering the expulsion of the Jews from the French colonies in 1685.

[435]   **Louis XIV, Roi de France et Navarre.** "Code Noir," in Mederic Louis Elie Moreau de Saint-Mery, *Loix et Constitutions des Colonies Francoises de l'Amerique sous le vent* (Paris, 1784), vol. I, pp. 414-24.

The text of the 'Black Code' ordering the expulsion of the Jews from the French colonies in 1685.

[436]   **Mederic Louis Elie Moreau de Saint-Mery.** *Loix et Constitutions des Colonies Francoises de l'Amerique sous le vent.* Paris, 1784. Vol. I,

pp. 12–15, 82–83, 180–81, 224–27, 266–67, 292–93, 388–89; vol. IV, pp. 850–53.

Laws and decrees concerning Jews in the French Caribbean.

[437] **J. Petitjean-Roget.** "Les Juifs a la Martinique sous l'Ancien Regime," *Revue d'Histoire des Colonies* (Paris), 43 (1956): 138–58.

Notes on Jewish life on Martinique before the French Revolution.

[438*] See no. 99, Pluchon, ed., *Histoire des Antilles et de la Guyane.*

A series of historical articles on the West Indies and the Guianas, with stress on French possessions.

[439] **Lowell Ragatz.** *Early French West Indian Records in the Archives Nationales,* Washington, 1941. 40 pp. (151–90).

Guide to documents in the French National Archives in Paris regarding the French colonies in the West Indies.

[440] **Jules Rennard.** "Juifs et Protestants aux Antilles Francaises au XVIIe siecle," *Revue d'Histoire des Missions* (Paris), 10:3 (Sept. 1933): 436–61.

Article describing the relations between Jews and Huguenots in the French West Indies.

[441] **L'Aurore St. Juste.** "Ancestres Pierre Mendes-France originaire d'Haiti," *Nouveau Monde* (Port-au-Prince), 12–13 July 1971, pp. 2–4.

A historical study on the Mendes-France family of Haiti.

[442] [Not used; see no. 417a.]

[443] **Jonathan H. Webster.** "The Merchants of Bordeaux in Trade to the French West Indies 1664–1717." Thesis, University of Minnesota, 1972.

The Jewish merchants of Bordeaux were actively involved in trade with their coreligionists in the West Indies.

XI

Trinidad

[444] **Gerard Besson.** *The Book of Trinidad.* Port of Spain, 1992. 422 pp.

An illustrated history of Trinidad, including some Jewish settlers and administrators.

[445] **Adrian Camps-Campins.** *The Seventh Birthday Party of Clara Rosa de Lima, St. Anns-Trinidad.* Port of Spain, 1989. 4 pp.

Description of a painting of a birthday celebration of a Spanish-Portuguese Jewish girl in Port of Spain.

[446*] See no. 19, Carmichael, *The History of the West Indian Islands.*

A detailed, comprehensive history of Trinidad, including the Jewish colonial administrator Daniel Hart.

[447] **Arthur De Lima.** *The De Limas of Frederick Street.* Port of Spain, 1975. 170 pp.

The history of the Spanish-Portuguese Jewish family De Lima of Port of Spain.

[448] **Arthur De Lima.** *The House of Jacob.* London, 1981. 463 pp.

A romanticized history of Jews in Trinidad.

[449] **Donna Farah.** "The Jewish Community in Trinidad 1930–1970." Thesis, University of the West Indies (St. Augustine), 1991. 46 pp.

Covers the Jewish history of Trinidad.

XII

General

[450] **I. Abrahams.** "Hebrew Loyalty under the First Four Georges," *TJHSE* (London), 9 (1918–1920): 103–30.

The attitude of the Jewish settlers in British colonies towards the British governors.

[451] **H. M. Alvares Correa.** *The Alvares Correa Families of Curaçao and Brazil.* Paris [The Hague], private publication, 1965. 60 pp.

Genealogical studies on the Portuguese Jewish family Alvares Correa in Curaçao, Coro, and Barranquilla.

[452] **Adam Anderson.** *An Historical and Chronological Deduction of the Origin of Commerce.* London, 1787-89. Vol. I, 556 pp.; vol. II, 647 pp.; vol. III, 568 pp.; vol. IV, 718 pp.

History of international commerce and the British, French, Dutch, and Danish interests in the West Indies.

[453] **Mordechai Arbell.** "Beit Saba Heritage — Sefardi Communities in Latin America," *Agudat Moreshet Beit Saba* (Tel Aviv), 3 Feb. 1977, pp. 38–43.

Family traditions of the Sephardi Jews in Latin America.

[454] **Mordechai Arbell.** *'La Nacion' — The Spanish and Portuguese Jews in the Caribbean.* Tel Aviv: Museum of the Jewish Diaspora, 1981. 49 pp.

Historical introduction to the museum's exhibition on Spanish-Portuguese Jews in the Caribbean.

[455] **Mordechai Arbell.** "Los Judios Hispano Portugueses del Caribe," *Sefardica* (Buenos Aires), no. 1 (1984): 85–93.

A short historical essay on the first Jewish settlers on the American continent.

[456] **Mordechai Arbell.** *Los djudios de España i Portugal en la filatelia mundial.* Jerusalem: Semana, 1988. 72 pp.

Historical essay on postage stamps honoring Spanish-Portuguese Jews, with special attention to stamps from Suriname, Barbados, Netherlands Antilles, Panama, and Venezuela.

[457] **Mordechai Arbell.** "1992: 500 Years after Columbus. The Spanish-Portuguese Nation of the Caribbean — La Nacion," in *Encyclopaedia Judaica Year Book 1990/91* (Jerusalem, 1992), pp. 12–25.

A concise historical essay on the Spanish-Portuguese Jews in the Caribbean, from their original settlement through today.

[458] **Mordechai Arbell.** "La 'Nacion Judia' Hispano-Portuguese del Caribe," *Sefardica* (Buenos Aires), no. 9 (Aug. 1992): 171–89.

An article commemorating 500 years of the expulsion of the Jews from Spain in 1492 and their settlement on the American continent.

[459] **Mordechai Arbell.** יהדות ספרד, סיפורה של קהילה ("Spanish Jews, a story of a community"). Jaffa: Israeli Post Philatelic Services, 1992. 21 pp.

Textbook, for schoolchildren, for the study of the history of the Spanish-Portuguese Jews through postage stamps.

[460] **Mordechai Arbell.** "1924–1660 תולדות משפחת לופז–פניה" ("The Annals of the Lopez-Penha Family 1660–1924"), *Peamim* (Jerusalem), 48 (1992): 117–34.

[461] **Mordechai Arbell.** "Inscriptions Juives dans les cimetieres des Caraibes" (Jerusalem, 1993). 176 pp. Manuscript in the possession of Mr. M. Arbell.

Compilation of inscriptions in Jewish cemeteries and synagogues in the Caribbean.

[462] **German Arciniegas.** *Biografia del Caribe.* Buenos Aires, 1945. 544 pp.

The story of the Caribbean area presented by a famous Colombian writer.

[462a] **João Lucio d'Azevedo.** *Historia dos Cristãos Novos Portugueses.* Lisbon, 1921 (reprinted 1945).

A history of the Portuguese conversos, this work also deals with the American continent.

[462b] **João Lucio d'Azevedo.** "Notas sobre o judaismo e a Inquisicao no Brasil," *Revista do Instituto Historico Geographico Brasileiro*, 145 (1922): 679–97.

Historical notes on the Jews and conversos in Brazil, based on documents of the Inquisition.

[463] **Violet Barbour.** "Privateers and Pirates of the West Indies," *American Historical Review*, 16 (1910–11): 529–66.

Illegal and illicit trade in the West Indies, at times sanctioned by the European powers.

[464] **Violet Barbour.** *Capitalism in Amsterdam in the Seventeenth Century*. Ann Arbor, 1963. 171 pp.

The commercial activities, including those of the Jews, between Amsterdam and the Dutch colonies on the American continent.

[465] **Richard D. Barnett.** "The Correspondence of the Mahamad of the Spanish and Portuguese Congregation of London during the Seventeenth and Eighteenth Centuries," *TJHSE* (London), 20 (1959/60): 1–50.

The article includes correspondence concerning Jews in Barbados and Jamaica.

[466] **Richard D. Barnett.** *The Bevis Marks Synagogue*. Oxford: Oxford University Press, 1970. 20 pp.

The story of the Spanish-Portuguese synagogue in London.

[467] **Richard D. Barnett.** *The Sephardi Heritage*. London: Vallentine, Mitchell and Co., 1971. 635 pp.

Observations on the history of Sephardi Jewry the world over.

[468] **Abraham Jehisquia Bassan.** *Sermoes Funebres as deploraveis memorias do muy insigne theologo, celebre pregador, Cabeça desta Naçaô, illustre . . . reverendissimo Sr. H.H.R. David Israel Athias, faleceo em 16 Adar Sheni 5513*. Amsterdam, 1753. 38 pp.

Funeral sermons for Rabbi David Israel Athias of Amsterdam, including references to Curaçao and Barbados. While Bassan is traditionally listed as the author, he is the second of the book's two principal authors, the first being Jahacob de Selomoh Hisquiau Saruco.

[469] Ralph G. Bennett. "Genealogical Resources from the Caribbean, available for Jewish Researchers," *Los Muestros* (Brussels), May 1994: 18–23.

[470] Yohanan Ben-Yitzhak. תשובת הגאונים ("The Response of the Knowledgeable"). Amsterdam, 1707. 36 pp.

Description of the difficulties in obtaining divorce papers from Jews who settled in the West Indies.

[471] Stephen Birmingham. *The Grandees*. New York: Dell Publishing Co., 1972. 309 pp.

A romanticized history of the Spanish-Portuguese Jews in New York.

[472] Herbert I. Bloom. "The Dutch Archives, with Special Reference to American Jewish History," *PAJHS*, 32 (1931): 7–21.

[473] Herbert I. Bloom. "A Study of Brazilian Jewish History 1623–1654, Based Chiefly upon the Findings of the Late Samuel Oppenheim," *PAJHS*, 33 (1934): 43–125.

[474] Herbert I. Bloom. *The Economic Activities of the Jews of Amsterdam in the Seventeenth and Eighteenth Centuries*. Williamsport, Pa., 1937. 332 pp.

A careful study describing Jewish economic life in Amsterdam in the 17th and 18th centuries, and the importance of commerce with the Caribbean.

[475] Günter Böhm. "The First Sephardic Cemeteries in South America and in the West Indies," *Studia Rosenthaliana* (Amsterdam), 25:1 (Spring 1951): 3–14.

Description of Jewish cemeteries in the West Indies.

[476] Günter Böhm. *Nuevos antecedentes para una historia de los Judios en Chile colonial*. Santiago de Chile: Editorial Universitaria, 1973. 134 pp.

Documentary history of the Jews in Chile during the Spanish colonial period.

[477] Günter Böhm. "La Vida Judia en Chile y en Peru durante el siglo XIX," in *Judaica Latinoamericana* [vol. 1] (Jerusalem, 1988), pp. 32–40.

Jewish life in Chile and Peru in the 19th century.

General

[478] **Günter Böhm.** *Los sefardies en los dominios holandeses de America del Sur y del Caribe 1630–1750.* Frankfurt-am-Main, 1992. 243 pp.

A study of the Spanish-Portuguese Jews in the Dutch colonies in the Caribbean and South America.

[479] **Günter Böhm.** "Las Primeras sinagogas Sefaradies en Sud America y en la area del Caribe," *Sefardica* (Bueno Aires), no. 9 (1992): 193–205.

Description of Spanish-Portuguese synagogues in Suriname and Curaçao.

[480] **Charles R. Boxer.** *The Dutch in Brazil 1624–1654.* Oxford, 1957. 327 pp.

A thorough history of the Dutch colony in Brazil for 30 years in the 17th century.

[481] **Charles R. Boxer.** *The Dutch Seaborne Empire 1600–1800.* London, 1965. 326 pp.

A historical account of Dutch colonial ventures on the American continent in the 17th and 18th centuries.

[482] **Frederic Brenner.** *Sephardi Itinerary 1992.* Tel Aviv: Museum of the Jewish Diaspora, 1992. 27 pp.

A photo-historical journey by a famous cameraman to Spanish-Portuguese Jewish communities throughout the world.

[483] **Carl** and **Roberta Bridenbaugh.** *No Peace Beyond the Line — the English in the Caribbean 1624–1690.* New York, 1972. 440 pp.

A detailed history on the British presence in the Caribbean in the 17th century.

[484*] See no. 243, Burns, *History of the British West Indies.*

[485*] See no. 302, Campbell, "Note on the Jewish Community of St. Thomas".

[486*] See no. 18, Cardozo de Bethencourt, "Notes on the Spanish and Portuguese Jews".

[487] **Eliakim Carmoly.** "Les Israelites des deux Indes (Indes Occidentales)," *Revue Orientale: Recueil Periodique d'Histoire, de Geographie et de Litterature* (Brussels), 3 (1843–1844): 134–38, 215–75.

Historical notes on Jews of the Caribbean.

[488] **Stanley F. Chyet.** *Lopez of Newport.* Detroit: Wayne State University Press, 1970. 246 pp.

A historical account of Aaron Lopez from Newport, Rhode Island, a shipowner and merchant with contacts in the West Indies.

[489] **Mario E. Cohen.** "Primeras sinagogas de America," *Sefardica* (Buenos Aires), no. 7 (1989): 143–46.

An account of the first Jewish synagogues on the American continent.

[490] **Mario E. Cohen.** *Bibliografia en idioma castellano del judaismo y criptojudaismo en America colonial.* Buenos Aires, 1990. 50 pp.

A Spanish-language bibliography on Jews and conversos in colonial (Spanish) America.

[491] **Martin A. Cohen.** "The Religion of Luis Rodriguez Carvajal," *AJA*, 20:1 (Apr. 1968): 33–62.

A biography of a famous converso martyr in Mexico, Luis de Carvajal.

[492] **Robert Cohen.** "Early Caribbean Jewry: A Demographic Perspective," *Jewish Social Studies*, 45:2 (1983): 123–34.

A study of the position of Jews in society in Martinique, Barbados, and Jamaica, and an attempt at drawing demographic conclusions regarding the Jewish settlements in the Caribbean.

[493] **Avraham Cohen de Herrera.** שער שמים ("Gate of God"). Amsterdam, 1655. 34 pp.

Introductory material by the translator includes description of the Jewish exodus from Brazil; this is the first publication in Hebrew mentioning Brazil. Main text translated from the Spanish by the chief Haham (Rabbi) of Brazil, Isaac Abohav da Fonseca.

[494*] See no. 248, Coke, *A History of the West Indies.*

[495] **Lambros Comitas.** *Caribbeana, 1900–1965: A Topical Bibliography.* Seattle, 1968. 909 pp.

Touches on all aspects of life and mores treated in publications on the Caribbean.

General

[496] **Alan Corre.** "The Sephardim of the U.S.," in *The Western Sephardim* (Grendon, Northants.: Gibraltar Books, 1989), pp. 384-430. (Vol. 2 of *The Sephardi Heritage*.)

On the first Jews in the United States.

[497] **S. Cortissoz.** "The Maduro Family," *Los Muestros* (Brussels), Mar. 1992: 21–23.

About the famous Spanish-Portuguese Maduro family in Curaçao, Panama, and Costa Rica.

[498] **David Brion Davis.** "The Slave Trade and the Jews," *New York Review of Books*, 41:21 (22 Dec. 1994): 14–16.

Discussion of the question of Jewish involvement or noninvolvement in the slave trade.

[499] [Not used; see no. 462a.]

[500] [Not used; see no. 462b.]

[501*] See no. 36, de Sola Pool, "The Mohelim of Curaçao and Surinam".

[502] **David de Sola Pool.** *Portraits Etched in Stone.* New York: Columbia University Press, 1952. 543 pp.

A complete list of inscriptions from the first Jewish cemeteries in New York, and a historical account of those buried in them.

[503] **David de Sola Pool.** *An Old Faith in the New World.* New York: Columbia University Press, 1955. 595 pp.

History of Spanish-Portuguese Jews in North America, written by the Haham (Rabbi) of the "Shearith Israel" congregation in New York.

[504] **J. G. van Dillen.** "De Economische Positie en Betekenis der Joden in de Republiek en in de Nederlandse Koloniale Wereld," in Hendrik Brugmans, ed., *Geschiedenis der Joden in Nederland* (Amsterdam, 1940), pp. 561–616.

An account of the Jews' economic role in the Dutch colonies and in Holland.

[505] **Judith Laikin Elkin.** *Imagining Idolatry: Missionaries, Indians and Jews.* Providence, R.I., 1992. 37 pp.

Interreligious relations in early colonial South America, and the Jews' role in them.

[506] **Leon H. Elmaleh.** *The Jewish Cemetery, Ninth and Spruce Streets.* Philadelphia, 1962. 30 pp.

A short history and list of the graves in the Spanish-Portuguese Jewish cemetery in Philadelphia.

[507] **Isaac Emmanuel.** "Fortunes and Misfortunes of the Jews in Brazil (1630–1654), *AJA*, Jan. 1955: 4–64.

An account of Jewish life in Dutch Brazil, based mainly on documents in Amsterdam archives.

[508] **Isaac Emmanuel.** "Seventeenth Century Brazilian Jewry, a Critical Review," *AJA*, 14:1 (Apr. 1962): 32–41.

On the Jewish congregations "Zur Israel" and "Magen Abraham" in Recife and Olinda in Brazil under Dutch rule.

[509] *Enciclopedia Judaica Castellana.* Mexico, 1948–51. 10 vols.

[510] *Encyclopaedia Judaica.* Berlin, 1928. 10 vols.

[511] *Encyclopaedia Sefardica Neerlandica.* Amsterdam, 1948–50. 2 vols. (No more published?)

[512] *Encyclopedie van de Nederlandse Antillen.* Amsterdam: Elsevier, 1969. 708 pp.

Encyclopedia on the Dutch Antilles, in which facets of Jewish presence and history appear several times. Edited by Dr. H. Hoetink.

[513] *Encyclopedie van de Nederlandse West Indie.* The Hague, 1914–17.

[514] **Eli Faber.** *A Time for Planting. The First Migration 1654–1820.* Baltimore, 1992. 188 pp. (Vol. 1 of series: The Jewish People in America.)

A story about the first Jewish settlers on the American continent.

[514a] **Maria Jose Pimenta Ferro Tavares.** *Os Judeus em Portugal No Seculo XV.* Lisbon: Universidad Nova de Lisboa, 1982. 533 pp.

The history of the Jews in Portugal on the advent of the Inquisition. A second volume was published in 1984.

[515] **E. Alvin Fidanque.** "Early Sephardic Jewish Settlers in North America and the Caribbean," *Journal of Reform Judaism* (New York), Fall 1978: 77–82.

An article on the Spanish-Portuguese Jewish settlers on the American continent.

[516*] See no. 216, Fortune, *Merchants and Jews*.

[517] **David Franco Mendes.** תולדות גדולי ישראל. תולדות החכם משה רפאל אגילר ז'ל. ("The History of the Late Haham Moshe Rafael Aguilar"). Berlin, 1784. Pp. 15–17.

A biography of a prominent religious leader who was one of the first of his kind to settle in the Americas (Dutch Brazil).

[518] **Lee M. Friedman.** *Rabbi Haim Isaac Carigal, his Newport Sermon and his Yale Portrait.* Boston: private publication, 1940. 43 pp.

Remarks on the stay in Newport, Rhode Island, of the emissary from the Holy Land, Haham (Rabbi) Rafael Hayim Isaac Carigal, who also stayed in Curaçao & Suriname, and then died in Barbados.

[519] **Lee M. Friedman.** "Some References to Jews in the 'Sugar Trade,'" *PAJHS*, 42 (1952–53): 305–309.

Description of Jewish predominance in the world sugar trade.

[520] **Mozes Heiman Gans.** *Memorbook: History of Dutch Jewry from the Renaissance to 1940.* Baarn, 1977. 851 pp.

History of Dutch Jewry, also covering Dutch Jews in the Caribbean.

[521] **Albert Gastmann.** *Historical Dictionary of the French and Netherlands Antilles.* Metuchen, N.J., 1978. 162 pp.

Dictionary of terminology used for Dutch and French possessions in the Caribbean, in which many unclear expressions are clarified.

[522] **Balthazar Gerbier.** *A Sommary Description Manifesting that Greater Profits are to bee done in the Hott then in the Could Parts off the Coast off America . . . Advertissement for Men Inclined to Plantations.* Rotterdam, 1660. 24 pp.

A publication designed to attract planters to the colonies in the Caribbean.

[523]   **Jose Antonio Gonsalves de Mello.** "A Nacao Judaica do Brasil Holandes," *Revista do Instituto Arqueologico, Historico e Geografico Penambucano* (Recife), 1976. (242 pp.)

A journal article describing the life of the Spanish-Portuguese Jews in Dutch Brazil.

[524]   **Jose Antonio Gonsalves de Mello.** "Primera comunidad Judia de America colonial 1630–1654," *Sefardica* (Buenos Aires), no. 5 (1986): 21–40.

On the settling of Jews in Brazil.

[525]   **Cornelis Ch. Goslinga.** *The Dutch in the Caribbean and on the Wild Coast 1580–1680.* Assen, 1971. 647 pp.

A detailed, documented, exceptionally well written history on the Dutch in the Caribbean and the Guianas, covering the years 1580–1680.

[526]   **Cornelis Ch. Goslinga.** *A Short History of the Netherlands Antilles and Surinam.* The Hague, 1979. 198 pp.

A history of the two main Dutch settlements in America — Suriname and Curaçao.

[527]   **Cornelis Ch. Goslinga.** "De Nederlandse Antillen en Suriname 1914–1941," *Algemene Geschiedenis der Nederlanden* (Amsterdam), 14 (1979): 400–406.

History of the Dutch Antilles and Suriname in the 19th and 20th centuries.

[528]   **Cornelis Ch. Goslinga.** *The Dutch in the Caribbean and in the Guianas, 1680–1791.* Assen, 1985. 712 pp.

A detailed, carefully researched history of the Dutch in the Caribbean and the Guianas during the period 1680–1791.

[529]   **Yosef Hacohen.** דברי הימים ("A History"). Amsterdam, 1733. 144 pp.

A rabbinical study in which Jewish settlement in the West Indies is mentioned.

[530*] See no. 152, Hamelberg, *De Nederlanders.*

A study of Dutch presence in the West Indies.

[531*] See no. 49, Harlow, ed., *Colonising Expeditions.*

General

[532] **J. Hartog.** "Jose Diaz Pimienta, Rogue Priest," *AJA* (Cincinnati), 34 (Nov. 1982): 153–63.

The story of a scoundrel who, posing as a Catholic priest and as a converted Jew, traveled throught Curaçao, Venzuela, Cuba, and Mexico — an article showing life and beliefs in the Spanish Main in the 17th century.

[533] **S. Q. Henriques.** "Special Taxation of the Jews," *TJHSE* (London), 9 (1922): 53–66.

The taxation on the Jews, particularly prevalent in Jamaica.

[534] **Philip Hanson Hiss.** *Netherlands America — The Dutch Territories in the West.* New York, 1943. 225 pp.

History of the Dutch presence in America.

[535] **Dr. H. Hoetink, ed.** *Encyclopedie van de Nederlandse Antillen.* Amsterdam: Elsevier, 1969. 708 pp.

See no. 512.

[536] *Honoring 1776 and Famous Jews in American History.* New York: Joseph Jacobs Organization, 1975. 19 pp.

[537] **Leon Hühner.** "Whence Came the First Jewish Settlers of New York?" *PAJHS*, no. 9 (1901): 75–86.

An article tracing the torturous route of the first group of Jews to settle in New Amsterdam (New York).

[538] **Albert M. Hyamson.** *The Sephardim of England.* London, 1951. 468 pp.

History of the Spanish-Portuguese Jews of England, also describing their numerous contacts with the West Indies.

[539] **Herbert Israel.** "Wandering in the Caribbean Area," *Los Muestros* (Brussels), Dec. 1994: 61–62.

An article on the wandering of the Portuguese Jews until they reached the Caribbean area.

[540] *The Jewish Encyclopedia.* New York/London, 1901. 12 vols.

[541] **Yosef Kaplan.** "המפגש המחודש עם היהדות. היהודים הספרדים והפורטוגלים במערב בראשית העת החדשה" ("The Reencounter with Judaism — The Spanish-Portuguese Jews in the West in the New Era), *From the East to the End of the West — Spanish Jews 1492–*

1992, Tel Aviv: Museum of the Jewish Diaspora, Winter 1992/93, pp. 45–83.

Article on the settlement of Spanish-Portuguese Jews in the West.

[542] **Meir Kayserling.** "The Earliest Rabbis and Jewish Writers of America," *PAJHS* (Waltham), 3 (1894): 13–20.

[543] **Meir Kayserling.** "Une Histoire de la Litterature Juive de Daniel Levi de Barrios," *Revue des Etudes Juives* (Paris), 92 (Jan.-Mar. 1896): 88–101.

A historical review of the poet Daniel Levi de Barrios' work, with mention of his stay in Tobago.

[544] **Max J. Kohler.** "Some Early American Zionist Projects," *PAJHS*, 8 (1900): 75–118.

[545] **George Alexander Kohut.** "Sketches of Jewish loyalty, bravery and patriotism in the South American colonies and the West Indies," in Simon Wolf, ed., *The American Jew as patriot, soldier and citizen* (Philadelphia, 1895), pp. 443–84.

[546] **Bertram Wallace Korn.** *The Early Jews of New Orleans.* Waltham, Mass.: American Jewish Historical Society, 1969. 382 pp.

History of the New Orleans Jews in which their West Indies origin is described.

[547] **Bertram Wallace Korn.** התעצמותו של הקיבוץ היהודי באמריקה ("The Period of Growth of Power of the Jews in America"). Jerusalem: Magnes Press, 1971. 381 pp.

History of the first Jews in the United States. Text in Hebrew; added title page in English: *American Jewry: the formative years.*

[548] **Franklin B. Krohn.** "The Search for the Elusive Caribbean Jews" (March 1992). 16 pp. Manuscript in the American Jewish Archives, Cincinnati.

A short essay on the Jews who reached the Caribbean, the reasons behind their move, and its consequences.

[549] **Joannes de Laet.** *L'Histoire du Nouveau Monde ou Description des Indes Occidentales.* Leyden, 1640. 632 pp.

History of the West Indies before the massive settlement of the Jews.

[550] **Anita Libman Lebeson.** *Jewish Pioneers in America 1492–1848.* New York: 1931. 372 pp.

The settlement of the Jews on the American continent, with emphasis on those settling in the U.S.A.

[551*] See no. 222, Lehmann, "Early Relations between American Jews and Eretz Yisrael".

[552] **Robert Leonard.** "The Maduro Family and Their Tokens," *The Shekel* (New York), 5:4 (1973): 22–24.

A numismatic article on the coins/tokens issued by the Maduro family to facilitate their trade in the West Indies.

[553] **B. H. Levy.** *Savannah's Old Jewish Community Cemeteries.* Macon, Georgia: Mercer University Press, 1983. 118 pp.

History of the first Jewish cemeteries in Savannah, Georgia, and inscriptions found in them.

[554] **Boleslao Lewin.** "Los Portugueses en Buenos Aires en el periodo colonial," *Sefardica* (Buenos Aires), no. 7 (1989): 17–40.

The Portuguese conversos in the southern part of Latin America.

[555] **Seymour B. Liebman.** "Research Problems in Mexican Jewish History," *AJHQ*, 54 (1964–65): 165–82.

Problems encountered while researching the activities of the Spanish Inquisition in Mexico.

[556] **Seymour B. Liebman, ed.** *The Enlightened — The Writings of Luis de Carvajal, El Mozo.* Coral Gables: University of Miami Press, 1967. 157 pp.

The biography and writings of a Jewish martyr, executed by the Spanish Inquisition in Mexico.

[557] **Seymour B. Liebman.** *Los Judios en Mexico y America Central.* Mexico, 1971. 481 pp.

Description of the settlement of Jews in Mexico and Central America under Spanish rule.

[558] **Seymour B. Liebman.** *The Inquisitors and the Jews of the New World.* Coral Gables: University of Miami Press, 1975. 224 pp.

An inquiry into the Inquisition in Mexico and other centers in Latin America.

[559] **Seymour B. Liebman.** "Tomas Trevino de Sobremonte, A Jewish Mexican Martyr," *Jewish Social Studies*, 42:1 (Winter 1980): 63–74.

The story of a Jewish martyr of the Spanish Inquisition in Mexico.

[560] **Seymour B. Liebman.** *New World Jewry, 1493–1825 — Requiem for the Forgotten.* New York, 1982. 271 pp.

Historical notes on Jewish conversos in Spanish-ruled Latin America.

[561] **Seymour B. Liebman.** *Requiem por los olvidados — los Judios Espanoles en America.* Madrid, 1984. 230 pp.

Translation into Spanish of *New World Jewry, 1493–1825 — Requiem for the Forgotten,* above.

[562] **Seymour B. Liebman.** "Religion y costumbres judias entre los marranos de nuevo mundo colonial," *Sefardica* (Buenos Aires), no. 5 (1986): 41–46.

The secret observance of Judaism and Jewish customs prevalent among the crypto-Jews from Spain and Portugal.

[563] **Seymour B. Liebman.** "The Secret Jewry in the Spanish New World Colonies 1500–1820," in *The Western Sephardim* (Grendon, Northants.: Gibraltar Books, 1989), pp. 474-96. (Vol. 2 of *The Sephardi Heritage.*)

The life of the conversos on the American continent under Spanish and Portuguese rule.

[564] **Elias Hiam Lindo.** *A Jewish Calendar.* London, 1838. 134 pp.

A calendar of events containing a chronological table of events in the Jewish settlement of the Caribbean from 1641.

[565] **Vida Lindo Guterman.** "Joshua Piza and His Descendants" (New York, 1967). 124 pp. Manuscript in the possession of Mr. Ricardo Henriquez, Miami, and Mr. M. Arbell.

A genealogical study of the family of a Curaçao cantor, taking the reader through St. Thomas, Panama, and Costa Rica.

[566] **Pablo Link.** *El Aporte Judio al descubrimiento de America.* Buenos Aires, 1974. 39 pp. (Issued as part of series: Biblioteca Popular Judia.)

On the Jewish origin of some of the Spanish discoverers of America.

[567] **Elias Lipiner.** *Gaspar da Gama, um Converso na Frota de Cabral.* Rio de Janeiro, 1987. 276 pp.

The story of a converso member among the crew of the Portuguese explorer Cabral.

[568] **Elias Lipiner.** *Izaque de Castro — o Mancebo que Veio Preso do Brasil.* Recife, 1992. 320 pp.

The history of the works and imprisonment of Isaque de Castro Tartas, a converso in Brazil.

[569] **Zvi Loker, ed.** *Jews in the Caribbean.* Jerusalem, 1991. 367 pp.

A collection of documents and comments on them, describing Jewish life in the Caribbean and the Guianas.

[570] **Zvi Loker.** "Conversos and Conversions in the Caribbean Colonies and Socio-Religious Problems of the Jewish Settlers," in *Judaica Latinoamericana* [vol. 1] (Jerusalem, 1988), pp. 20–31.

The religious problems encountered by the Jews settling in the Caribbean.

[571] **Moises Lopez Penha,** "Historia de la Familia Lopez Penha Tomada del Manuscrito, Traducido del Portugues por David Lopez Penha, continuada hasta 1927" (Santo Domingo, 1927). 18 pp. Manuscript in the possession of Mr. M. Arbell.

A manuscript describing the history of the Lopez-Penha family whose members lived as marranos in Spain and Portugal and as Jews in Izmir and Amsterdam, and which ultimately settled in Curaçao, Barranquilla, Maracaibo, and Santo Domingo.

[572] **David Macpherson.** *Annals of Commerce.* London, 1805. Vol. I, 719 pp.; vol. II, 738 pp.; vol. III, 728 pp.; vol. IV, 550 pp.

A historical work on the commercial interests of the colonial powers, and the settlement of Jews in the West Indies as part of those interests.

[573] **Jacob Rader Marcus.** "The West India and South America Expedition of the American Jewish Archives," *AJA* (Cincinnati), 5:1 (1953): 5–21.

A report by a group of scholars from the American Jewish Archives on their trip to Jewish sites in the Caribbean and the Guianas.

[574] **Jacob Rader Marcus.** Review of *The Sephardim of England* by Albert M. Hyamson, *AJA*, 5:2 (1953): 126–29.

See no. 538 for the book being reviewed.

[575] **Jacob Rader Marcus.** *American Jewry: Documents; 18th Century.* Cincinnati, 1959. 492 pp.

Authentic documents on American Jews in the 18th century, including those on their contacts with Jamaica, Barbados, Curaçao, Suriname, and Martinique.

[576] **Jacob Rader Marcus.** מבוא לתולדות יהדות אמריקה בתקופת ראשיתה ("Introduction to Early American Jewish History"). Jerusalem: Magnes Press, 1971. 317 pp.

History of the first Jews on the American continent, mainly in the United States.

[577] **Simeon J. Maslin.** "Toward the Preservation of Caribbean Jewish Monuments," *AJHQ*, 58 (1969): 472–83.

Description of Jewish sites in the Caribbean.

[578] **Samuel Augustus Mathews.** *The Lying Hero, or, an Answer to J. B. Moreton's Manners and Customs in the West Indies.* St. Eustatius, 1793. 160 pp.

A detailed description and defense of the behavior of white planters in the West Indies, their culture, mores, treatment of slaves, and their ethics, in response to Moreton's criticism. Mathews offers a very positive appraisal of the role of the Jews in the region.

[579] **Henry Mechoulan**, directeur. *Les Juifs d'Espagne, Histoire d'une diaspora 1492–1992.* Paris, 1992. 721 pp.

A series of articles by different authors on the Spanish Jewish Diaspora.

[580] **Ronald Mendes Chumaceiro.** "Mendes Chumaceiro Family Ancestral Charts," (Caracas, 1983). 13 pp. Manuscript in the possession of Mr. M. Arbell.

Genealogical study on the Mendes Chumaceiro Family in Amsterdam, Curaçao, Panama, and Venezuela.

[581] **Gordon Merrill.** "The Role of the Sephardic Jews in the British Caribbean Area," *Caribbean Studies* (San Juan), 4:1 (Apr. 1964): 32–49.

A comprehensive article on the impact of the Jewish population on life in the British Caribbean.

[582] **Allan Metz.** "'Those of the Hebrew Nation...' — The Sephardic Experience in Colonial Latin America," *AJA*, 44:1 (1992): 209–34.

The life of the Spanish Jews in part of Latin America under Spanish rule.

[583] **Victor A. Mirelman.** "Sephardim in Latin America after Independence," *AJA*, 44:1 (1992): 235–65.

Notes on Spanish Jews in certain Latin American countries after their liberation from Spain.

[584] **Sir Harold Mitchell.** *Europe in the Caribbean.* Stanford, Calif., 1963. 211 pp.

Description of the economic interests of the European powers in the Caribbean region.

[585] **Gerard Nahon.** "Une source pour l'histoire de la diaspora Sefarade au XVIIIe siecle: Le Copiador de Cartas — de la communaute Portugaise d'Amsterdam," in *The Sephardi and Oriental Jewish Heritage* (Jerusalem, 1982), pp. 109–22.

An article stressing the importance of the "Copiador de Cartas" as a source for studying the history of the Portuguese Jews in the 18th century, including mentions of correspondence with Caracas, St. Eustatius, Suriname, and Barbados.

[586] **Gerard Nahon.** "Les Relations entre Amsterdam et Constantinople au XVIII siecle d'apres le Copiador de Cartas de la Nation Juive Portugaise d'Amsterdam," in *Dutch Jewish History: proceedings of the symposium...1982* (Jerusalem, 1984), pp. 157–85.

On the relations between Spanish Jews in Amsterdam and those of Istanbul, based on Amsterdam Jewish Archives, including notes on Curaçao.

[587] **Gerard Nahon.** *Metropoles et peripheries Sefarades d'Occident.* Paris, 1993. 493 pp.

Description of Spanish Jewish centers in Western countries.

[588] **Aubrey Newman.** "The Sephardim of the Caribbean," in *The Western Sephardim* (Grendon, Northants.: Gibraltar Books, 1989), pp. 445–73. (Vol. 2 of *The Sephardi Heritage*.)

Short notes on Jewish life in the Caribbean.

[589] **New York Public Library.** "List of Works in the New York Public Library relating to the History and Condition of the Jews in Various Countries," *Bulletin of the New York Public Library* (New York), 17:7 (July 1913): 537–86, 17:8 (Aug. 1913): 611–64, 17:9 (Sept. 1913): 713–64.

Bibliographical notes on the books available in the New York Public Library on the Jews in the West Indies.

[590] **Johan Nieuhof.** "Voyages and travels into Brasil and the East Indies," in *A Collection of Voyages and Travels* (London, 1704), vol. 2, pp. 1–369.

Narrative by an officer of the Dutch army in Brazil, which contains a description of Jewish life in Brazil and the Jewish participation in the Dutch army.

[591] **Anita Novinsky.** "Sephardim in Brazil — The New Christians," in *The Western Sephardim* (Grendon, Northants.: Gibraltar Books, 1989), pp. 431–44. (Vol. 2 of *The Sephardi Heritage*.)

On the life of the conversos in Portuguese Brazil.

[592] **Anita Novinsky.** "Cripto-Judios en Sao-Paulo y el Sur de Brazil," *Sefardica* (Buenos Aires), no. 7 (1989): 63–68.

On conversos in Sao Paulo and southern Brazil.

[593] **Anita Novinsky.** "Los Sefardies en Brazil colonial: Los Nuevos Cristianos," *Sefardica* (Buenos Aires), no. 9 (Aug. 1992): 155–95.

Further information on the life of the conversos in Portuguese Brazil.

[594] **Salomon ben David de Oliveira.** שרשרות גבלות ("The Chain"). Amsterdam, 1665. 151 pp.

Notes on Isaque de Castro Tartas, martyr of the Portuguese Inquisition in Brazil.

[595] **Vere Langford Oliver.** *The Monumental Inscriptions of the British West Indies.* Dorchester, England, 1927. 267 pp.

Inscriptions from various cemeteries, including the Jewish ones but without the Hebrew text.

[596] **Samuel Oppenheim.** "The Early History of the Jews in New York 1654–1664," *PAJHS*, 18 (1909): 1–92.

History of the first Jewish settlers in New York.

[597] **Samuel Oppenheim.** "A List of Jews Made Denizens in the Reigns of Charles II and James II 1661–1687," *PAJHS*, 20 (1911): 109–13.

[598] **Samuel Oppenheim.** "List of Wills of Jews in the British West Indies prior to 1800," *PAJHS*, 32 (1931): 55–64.

List of Jewish signatories to wills made in Jamaica, Barbados, and Nevis.

[599] **Fred. Oudschans Dentz.** "Lucien Wolf en de Joodsche Kolonisatie in West Indie," *WIG* (Amsterdam), 12 (1930): 560–61.

Critical remarks on Lucien Wolf's publication on the Jewish settlement in the West Indies.

[600] **Richard Pares.** *War and Trade in the West Indies 1739–1763.* Oxford, 1936. 631 pp.

An economic analysis of trade relations and competition among European powers in the West Indies.

[601] **Richard Pares.** *Yankees and Creoles. The Trade between North America and the West Indies before the American Revolution.* Cambridge, Mass., 1956. 168 pp.

On the trade relations between North America and the West Indies, with statistical data included.

[602] **J. H. Parry, Philip Sherlock,** and **Anthony Maingot.** *A Short History of the West Indies.* New York, 1987. 333 pp.

Short historical notes on the West Indies.

[603] **N. Taylor Phillips.** "Items Relating to the History of the Jews of New York," *PAJHS* (Waltham), 11 (1903): 149–62.

[604] [Not used; see no. 514a.]

[605] **Angel Pulido Fernandez.** *Españoles sin patria y la raza sefardi.* Madrid, 1905 (reprinted Granada, 1993). 659 pp.

A monumental study on the situation of the Sephardic Diaspora at the end of the 19th century.

[606] **Abbe Raynal.** *A Philosophical and Political History of the Settlements and Trade of the Europeans in the East and West Indies.* London, 1788. Vol I, 399 pp.; vol. II, 426 pp.; vol. III, 432 pp.; vol.

IV, 253 pp.; vol. V, 499 pp.; vol. VI, 520 pp.; vol. VII, 564 pp.; vol. VIII, 458 pp.

A monumental historical work which details, among other topics, the history of the West Indies, including interesting accounts on the Jews in Brazil, Suriname, and Jamaica.

[607] **Mordecai Zeev Razin.** תולדות היהודים באמריקה—הקורות אשר עברו עליהם מראשית התישבותם בה עד ימינו אלה ("The History of the Jews of America from the First Years of Settlement to Our Days"). Warsaw, 1902. 203 pp.

A short history of the Jews on the American continent.

[608] **Isaac Rivkind.** "Some Remarks about Messengers from Palestine to America," *PAJHS*, 34 (1937): 288–94.

Description of the contact between the Holy Land and the Spanish-Portuguese Jews in America.

[609*] See no. 192, Rodway, *The West Indies and the Spanish Main*.

A description of the Jewish settlement in the West Indies in a general historical research work on the region.

[610] **Ludwig Rosenthal.** *La Participation Judia en el descubrimiento de America*. Bogota: B'nai B'rith, 1979. 146 pp.

The participation of Jews in the discoveries of the New World.

[611] **Cecil Roth.** *A History of the Marranos*. Philadelphia: Jewish Publication Society, 1953. 424 pp.

A history of the converso Diaspora throughout the world, in which there are references to the Jewish settlement on the American continent.

[612] **Mario Javier Saban.** *Judios Conversos. Vol. 1: Los Antepasados Judios de las familias tradicionales Argentinas*. Buenos Aires, 1990. 437 pp. (Series in progess; this is the first of three volumes issued to date.)

History of the converso families and their participation in the early history of Argentina.

[613] **Roberto Schopflocher.** "Vigencia de la Inquisicion," *Coloquio* (Buenos Aires), 25 (1993): 79–90.

Description of the Inquisition in Latin America.

[614] **Haim Shabethai.** תורת חיים ("Study of Life"). Salonika, 1722. 192 pp.

Documentary description of Responsa (questions and answers) on rabbinical laws; the work contains one from Brazil to Salonika, about whether to say certain prayers for rain in the American southern hemisphere, with its inverted seasons.

[615] **H. Sommerhausen.** "Die Geschichte der Niederlassung der Juden in Holland und in den niederländischen Kolonien," *MGWJ* (Breslau), 2 (1853): 121–45.

Historical notes on Dutch Jews and Jews in the Dutch colonies.

[616] **Isaiah Sonne.** "Jewish Settlement in the West Indies," *PAJHS*, 37 (1947): 353–67.

Notes on a 1773 report of a Jewish settlement in the West Indies.

[617] **Malcolm H. Stern.** *Americans of Jewish Descent.* Cincinnati: Hebrew Union College, 1960. 305 pp.

Genealogical studies and tables on the first Jewish families in the United States, some of them of Caribbean origin.

[618] **Malcolm H. Stern.** "Portuguese Sephardim in the Americas," *AJA*, 44:1 (1992): 141–78.

Notes on the settlement of Spanish-Portuguese Jews on the American continent.

[619] **Malcolm H. Stern.** "Notes on the Follow-up of the Jews of Recife" (New York, 1993). Manuscript; for further information contact Mr. M. Arbell.

A genealogical follow-up on Jewish families which left Recife 1650–1655 and dispersed in the Caribbean region.

[620] **Malcolm Stern** and **Bernard Postal.** *American Airlines Tourist's Guide to Jewish History in the Caribbean.* New York, 1962. 96 pp.

Historical background in a tourist-oriented guidebook to Jewish sites in the Caribbean.

[621] **Daniel M. Swetschinski.** "Conflict and Opportunity in 'Europe's other sea' — The Adventure of Caribbean Jewish Settlement," *AJH*, 72 (1982): 212–40.

Historical notes on the Jewish settlement in the Caribbean islands.

[622] **Benjamin Teensma.** "Los Judios y la opinion publica en el Brasil Holandes del siglo XVII," *Sefardica* (Buenos Aires), no. 7 (1989): 41–62.

The economic impact of Jews on life in Holland and the Dutch colonies. See also Teensma's "Resentment in Recife: Jews and public opinion in 17th-century Dutch Brazil," in Jan Lechner, ed., *Essays on cultural identity in colonial Latin America* (Leiden, 1988), 63–78.

[623] **Eva Alexandra Uchmany.** "El Judaismo de los Cristianos nuevos de origen Portugues en la Nueva Espana (Mexico y America Central)," *Sefardica* (Buenos Aires), no. 9 (1992): 207–20.

Concerns Portuguese conversos and their Judaism in Mexico and Central America. The reader is also directed to Eva Uchmany's several full-length books.

[624] **Peter Wiernik.** *History of the Jews in America.* New York: The Jewish History Publishing Co., 1931. 465 pp.

A historical work on the settlement of Jews on the American continent.

[625] **Geoffrey Wigoder.** "Jews of the Caribbean—between the old and the new," *The Jewish Chronicle Magazine* (London), 25 Mar. 1984, pp. 37–41.

An article on the Jews of the Caribbean following the "La Nacion" exhibition in the Museum of the Jewish Diaspora.

[626] **Geoffrey Wigoder.** "התפוצה הספרדית במאות ה19 וה20" ("The Sephardic Diaspora in the 19th and 20th Centuries"), in *From the East to the End of the West — Spanish Jews 1492–1992* (Tel Aviv: Museum of the Jewish Diaspora, Winter 1992/3), pp. 127–67.

An article on the Spanish-Portuguese Jewish Disapora the world over in the 19th and 20th centuries.

[627] **Samuel Wilson.** "Caribbean Diaspora," *Natural History*, 102:3 (Mar. 1993): 54–60.

A short article on the Jewish settlement in the Caribbean.

[628] **Arnold Wiznitzer.** "The Minute Book of Congregations Zur Israel of Recife and Magen Abraham of Mauricia, Brazil," *AJHQ,* 42 (1952–53): 217–93.

Historical article on the Jews of Dutch Brazil based on the archives of the Jewish communities in Recife and Olinda.

[629] **Arnold Wiznitzer.** "The Members of the Brazilian Jewish Community (1648–1653)," *PAJHS,* 42 (1952–53): 387–95.

Description of the Jewish families in Dutch Brazil.

[630] **Arnold Wiznitzer.** *The Records of the Earliest Jewish Community in the New World.* New York: American Jewish Historical Society, 1954. 108 pp.

Documentary evidence on the Jews in Dutch Brazil.

[631] **Arnold Wiznitzer.** "The Exodus from Brazil and Arrival in New Amsterdam of the Jewish Pilgrim Fathers, 1654," *PAJHS,* 44 (1954–55): 80–97.

The story of the arrival of the Jews from Dutch Brazil in New Amsterdam (New York).

[632] **Arnold Wiznitzer.** "The Synagogue and Cemetery of the Jewish Community in Recife, Brazil (1630–1654)," *PAJHS,* 44 (1954–55): 126–30.

Data on the Jewish sites of Dutch Brazil which do not exist today.

[633] **Arnold Wiznitzer.** "Jewish Studies in Dutch Brazil 1630–1654," *PAJHS,* 46 (1956–57): 40–50.

Description of Jewish intellectual life in Dutch Brazil.

[634] **Arnold Wiznitzer.** "Isac de Castro — Brazilian Jewish Martyr," *PAJHS,* 47 (1957–58): 63–75.

The history and martyrdom of Isaque de Castro Tartas, victim of the Portuguese Inquisition in Brazil.

[635] **Arnold Wiznitzer.** *Jews in Colonial Brazil.* New York: Columbia University Press, 1960. 227 pp.

A basic history of the Jews in Dutch Brazil.

[636] **Arnold Wiznitzer.** "Crypto Jews in Mexico during the sixteenth century," *PAJHS,* 51 (1961–62): 168–216.

Notes on the Jewish conversos in Mexico in the 16th century.

[637] **Arnold Wiznitzer.** "Crypto Jews in Mexico during the seventeenth century," *AJHQ,* 51 (1961–62): 222–68.

Notes on the Jewish conversos in Mexico in the 17th century.

[638*]   See no. 128, Wolf, "American Elements".

A brief article on Jewish settlement in America, including the West Indies.

[639]   **Lucien Wolf.** "Jews of Tudor England", in his *Essays in Jewish History*, ([London:] The Jewish Historical Society of London, 1934), pp. 71–90.

A study on prominent Jews in Tudor England, including those who came from the West Indies.

[640]   **Egon** and **Frieda Wolff.** "The Provenance of the First Jews in New Amsterdam" 19 pp. Manuscript in the American Jewish Archives, Cincinnati.

Analysis of the different theories on the wanderings of the first group of Jews who settled in New Amsterdam.

[641]   **Egon** and **Frieda Wolff.** *Judeus no Brasil Imperial.* Sao Paulo: Centro de Estudos Judaicos, Universidade de Sao Paulo, 1975. 549 pp.

History of the Jews in colonial Brazil.

[642]   **Egon** and **Frieda Wolff.** *A Odisseia dos Judeus de Recife.* Sao Paulo: Centro de Estudos Judaicos, Universidade de Sao Paulo, 1979. 342 pp.

Destinations of the Dutch Jews after expulsion from Dutch Brazil, 1654.

[643]   **Egon** and **Frieda Wolff.** *Dicionario Biografico. Vol. 1: Judaizantes e Judeus no Brasil 1500–1808.* Rio de Janeiro, 1986. 222 pp. (Series in progress; this is the first of seven volumes issued to date.)

Analysis of the families of Jews and conversos in Brazil.

[644]   **Egon** and **Frieda Wolff.** *Judeus, Judaizantes e seus Escravos.* Rio de Janeiro, 1987. 55 pp.

Jews, conversos, and their slaves in Brazil.

[645]   **Egon** and **Frieda Wolff.** *Quantos Judeus Estiveram no Brasil Holandes.* Rio de Janeiro, 1991. 131 pp.

A study of different theories on the number of Jews in Dutch Brazil.

[646]   **Abraham Yaari.** *Les Emissaires de la Terre Sainte. Histoire de la mission du pays vers la diaspora depuis la destruction du Second*

Temple jusq'au XIX siecle (in Hebrew). Jerusalem, 1951 (reprinted 1977). 12 pp.

On the messengers from the Holy Land to the Jewish Diaspora, including those who went to the American continent. This text originally appeared as: Abraham Yaari, שלוחי ארץ ישראל בתירייא. ירושלים חש"י. in Simha Assaf, ed., *Minhah li-Yehudah, mugash leha-Rav Yehudah Leb Zlotnik* (Jerusalem, 1949), pp. 212-225.

Author/Title Index

A

"About the Savan Jewish Cemetery." SEE Baa, Enid M.

Abrahams, I. "Hebrew Loyalty," **450**

Abrams, Monty R. SEE Relkin, Stanley T., and Monty R. Abrams

"Abrege de l'histoire de Tobago." SEE Klopmann, Ewald von

Abstract of all the Statutes made concerning aliens. SEE Hayne, Samuel

"Acercamiento a la obra de Daniel Lopez Laguna." SEE Cabezas Alguacil, Concepcion

Acosta Saignes, Miguel. *Historia de los Portugueses en Venezuela,* **340**

"Additional Notes on the History of the Jews of Barbados." SEE Davis, N. Darnell

"Additional Notes on the History of the Jews of Surinam." SEE Roos, J. S.

"Adventure of Caribbean Jewish Settlement." SEE Swetschinski, Daniel M., "Conflict and Opportunity," **621**

Agudo Freites, Raul. *Elias David Curiel,* **341**

Ainbinder, Pierre. "Report on Journey to Belize City, Belize — Visit to the Jewish Burial Ground," **374**

Aizenberg, Isidoro. "Die or Leave: An Anti-Jewish Riot," **345**

———. "Dos Commerciantes Judios de la Epoca Colonial," **344**

———. "The 1855 Expulsion of the Curaçaoan Jews," **346**

———. "Judios en la Caracas del 1800," **342**

———. "Venezuela y los Judios Venezuelanos," **343**

Alexander Hamilton. SEE Schachner, Nathan

"Alexander Hamilton's West Indian Boyhood." SEE Lewisohn, Florence

"Algunas acciones de los Holandeses en la region." SEE Felice Cardot, Carlos

Alland, Alexander. "Jews of the Virgin Islands," **296**

Altman, P. "Bridgetown Synagogue Restoration Report," **198**

Alvares Correa, H. M. "The Alvares Correa Families," **451**

"The Alvares Correa Families." SEE Alvares Correa, H. M.

American Airlines Tourist's Guide to Jewish History. SEE Stern, Malcolm H., and Bernard Postel
"American Elements in the Resettlement." SEE Wolf, Lucien
American Jewry: Documents. SEE Marcus, Jacob Rader
American Jewry: The Formative Years. SEE Korn, Bertram Wallace, "The Period of Growth of Power," **547**
Americans of Jewish Descent. SEE Stern, Malcolm H.
"Analysis of Annals Relating to the Early Jewish Settlement." SEE Rens, L. L. E.
"Ancestres Pierre Mendes-France." SEE St. Juste, L'Aurore
"Ancient Jewish community in Curaçao" (in Hebrew). SEE Beller, Yaakov
Anderson, Adam. *An Historical and Chronological Deduction of the Origin of Commerce,* **452**
Andrade, Jacob A. P. M. *A Record of the Jews in Jamaica,* **237**
Andrews, Evangeline Walker, ed. SEE Schaw, Janet, *Journal of a Lady of Quality,* **193a**
"Anglo-Dutch Relations from 1660 to 1688." SEE Deen, Lucille D.
Annals of Commerce. SEE Macpherson, David
"Annals of the Lopez-Penha Family" (in Hebrew). SEE Arbell, Mordechai
Aporte Judio al descubrimiento. SEE Link, Pablo
Arauz Monfante, Celestino Andres. *El Contrabando Holandes en el Caribe,* **347**

Arbell, Mordechai [Mordehay]. "Annals of the Lopez-Penha Family" (in Hebrew), **460**
———. "Beit Saba Heritage — Sefardi Communities," **453**
———. *Djudios de España i Portugal en la filatelia,* **456**
———. "Dona Sara de Coro, Venezuela," **348**
———. "Failure of the Jewish Settlement in the Island of Tobago," **3**
———. "Historia de la familia Lopez-Penha 1660–1924, **397**
———. "Inscriptions Juives dans les cimetieres," **461**
———. "La Istoria de los Sefardis en las Islas de Martinique, Guadeloupe," **405**
———. "Jewish Community of St. Eustatius" (in Hebrew), **174**
———. "Judios Hispano Portugueses del Caribe," **455**
———. "Mordehay Ricardo en Timbro," **349**
———. *"La Nacion",* **454**
———. "La 'Nacion Judia'," **458**
———. "1992: 500 Years after Columbus," **457**
———. "Sefaradis de Pauroma," **1**
———. "Sefaradis i el dezvelopamiento . . . de Sud-Amerika," **2**
———. "Spanish Jews, a story" (in Hebrew), **459**
Arbell, Mordechai, and **Barouh Lionarons.** "Jerusalem aan de Suriname rivier," **4**
"Archeological Investigation at Joden Savanne." SEE Mitrasingh, Benjamin S.

Architektuur van Surinam. SEE Temminck Groll, C. L., and A. R. H. Tjin a Djie

Archives Nationales, Paris. "List of Properties Situated in Saint Domingue," **406**

Arciniegas, German. *Biografia del Caribe,* **462**

Arjona, Nadhji. *Bob Eisenman Brandon,* **375**

———. *La familia Fidanque . . . The Fidanque Family,* **377**

———. "Raices Centenares del Pueblo Hebreo en la Republica de Panama," **376**

"Aspects of the Economic, Religious and Social History of the 18th Century Jamaican Jews." SEE Zager, Melvin R.

Attema, Yipie. *St. Eustatius, Historical Gem of the Caribbean,* **175**

August, Thomas G. "Family Structure and Jewish Continuity in Jamaica," **240**

———. "Jewish Assimilation and the Plural Society in Jamaica," **238**

———. Review of *Minorities and Power in a Black Society,* by Carol S. Holzberg, **239**

d'Azevedo, João Lucio. *Historia dos Cristãos Novos,* **462a**

———. "Judeus de Surinam," **4a**

———. "Notas sobre o judaismo e a Inquisicao," **462b**

B

Baa, Enid M. "About the Savan Jewish Cemetery," **299**

———. "The Preservation of the Sephardic Records of the Island of St. Thomas, Virgin Islands," **297**

———. "Sephardic Communities in the Virgin Islands," **298**

Bailey, Wilma R. "Social control in the Preemancipation Society of Kingston," **241**

Bakker, Eveline, Leo Dulhuisen, and Mauritz Massankhan. *Geschiedenis van Suriname,* **5**

Barata, Mario. "A Nacao Judaica Portuguesa do Surinam a e sua relacoes com o Brazil no seculo XVIII," **6**

"Barbados Census of 1680." SEE Dunn, Richard S.

Barbour, Violet. *Capitalism in Amsterdam,* **464**

———. "Privateers and Pirates," **463**

Barnett, Richard D. *Bevis Marks Synagogue,* **466**

———. "Correspondence of the Mahamad," **465**

———. *Sephardi Heritage,* **467**

———. "Tombstones in Barbados," **199**

Baron, Jose Watnik. SEE Bermudez, Dino Manco, and Jose Watnik Baron

Barre, Antoine Joseph Le Febvre de la. *Description de la France Equinoctiale.* SEE La Barre

———. *Relation de ce qui s'est passe dans les Isles et Terre Ferme de l'Amerique.* SEE Clodore, Jean de

Barrios, Daniel Levi de. SEE Levi de Barrios, Daniel

Barrios, Miguel de. SEE Levi de Barrios, Daniel

Bassan, Abraham Jehisquia. *Sermoes Funebres,* **468**

Beckles, Hilary. *A History of Barbados: from Amerindian Settlement to Nation-State,* **200**

"Beginnings of British Guyana." SEE Davis, N. Darnell

"Beit Saba Heritage — Sefardi Communities." SEE Arbell, Mordechai

Belinfante, Frederik Jozef. *Geneology of the Belinfante Family,* **201**

Beller, Yaakov. "The Ancient Jewish community in Curaçao" (Hebrew), **133**

Bellin, Jacques Nicolas. *Description Geographique de la Guyanne,* **9**

Bennett, Ralph G. "Genealogical Resources," **469**

———. "Jews of Exotic Surinam and Their History," **10**

Ben-Yitzhak, Yohanan. "Response of the Knowledgeable" (in Hebrew), **470**

Bermudez, Dino Manco, and Jose Watnik Baron. *Nuestras Gentes,* **350**

Beschrijving van de Plechtigheden nevens de Lofdichten en Gebeden, uitgesproken op het eerste Jubelfeest . . . op de Savane. SEE Dornsberg, Hendrick Willem, and Cornelius Dornsberg.

Beschrijving van Suriname. SEE Sypesteyn, C. A. van

Beschryving van Guiana of de Wilde Kust in Zuid-America. SEE Hartsinck, Jan Jacob

Besson, Gerard. *Book of Trinidad,* **444**

"Between Amsterdam and New Amsterdam." SEE Yerushalmi, Hayim Yosef

Bevis Marks Synagogue. SEE Barnett, Richard

Bibliografia en idioma castellano del judaismo. SEE Cohen, Mario E.

Biet, Antoine. *Voyage de la France equinoxiale en l'isle de Cayenne entrepris par les Francois en l'annee M.DC.LII,* **11, 409**

Bijlsma, R. "De Brieven van Gouveneur van Aerssen van Sommelsdijk," **13**

———. "David de Is. C. Nassy, Author of the *Essai Historique sur Surinam,*" **13a**

———. "De stichting van de Portugeesch-Joodsche gemeente en Synagoge in Suriname," **12**

Bille, Frants Ernest. "Manner in which Believers in the Mosaic Faith," **300**

"Biografia de Dr Mordechai Ricardo." SEE de Pool, John

Biografia del Caribe. SEE Arciniegas, German

Birmingham, Stephen. *The Grandees,* **471**

Bloch, Harry. "David D'Isaac Nassy, M.D., 1748 (?) to 1806," **14**

Blome, Richard. *Description of the Island of Jamaica,* **202**

Bloom, Herbert I. "Dutch Archives," **472**

———. *Economic Activities of the Jews,* **474**

———. "A Study of Brazilian Jewish History," **473**

Blyden, Edward. *The Jewish Question,* **301**

Author/Title Index

Bob Eisenman Brandon. SEE Arjona, Nadhji
Böhm, Günter. "First Sephardic Cemeteries," 475
———. *Nuevos antecedentes,* 476
———. "Las Primeras sinagogas Sefaradies," 479
———. *Los sefardies en los dominios holandeses,* 478
———. "Synagogues of Surinam," 15
———. "Vida Judia en Chile y en Peru," 477
Bolingbroke, Henry. *A Voyage to the Demerary,* 16
Book of Trinidad. SEE Besson, Gerard
Book Review. SEE Review
Boucher, Philip P. *Nouvelles Frances,* 410
Boxer, Charles R. *The Dutch in Brazil 1624–1654,* 480
———. *The Dutch Seaborne Empire,* 481
Brenner, Frederic. *Sephardi Itinerary 1992,* 482
Bridenbaugh, Carl and **Roberta.** *No peace beyond the line,* 483
"Bridgetown, Barbados." SEE Coleman, Edward D.
"Bridgetown Synagogue Restoration Report." SEE Altman, P.
"De Brieven van Gouveneur van Aerssen van Sommelsdijk." SEE Bijlsma, R.
Brutus, Edner. *Revolution dans Saint Domingue,* 411
Bubberman, F. C. SEE Koeman, C., ed., 59
Buddingh', Bernard R. *Van Punt en Snoa,* 134

Bueno de Mesquita, J. A., and **Fred. Oudschans Dentz.** *Geschiedkundige tijdtafel van Suriname,* 17
"The Burial Society of Curaçao in 1783." SEE de Sola Pool, David
Burns, Sir Alan. *History of the British West Indies,* 243, 484
Butel-Dumont, Georges-Marie. *Histoire et commerce des Antilles Angloises,* 202a, 242a

C

Cabezas Alguacil, Concepcion. "Acercamiento a la obra de Daniel Lopez Laguna," 244
Cadbury, Henry J. "Quakers, Jews and Freedom of Teaching," 203
Cahen, Abraham. "Les Juifs dans les colonies francaises," 412
———. "Les Juifs de la Martinique," 413
"Camille Pissarro, St. Thomas." SEE Paiewonsky, Isidor
Campbell, Albert. A. "Note on the Jewish Community of St. Thomas," 302, 485
Campbell, P. F. *An Outline of Barbados History,* 204
Camps-Campins, Adrian. *The Seventh Birthday Party,* 445
Capitalism in Amsterdam. SEE Barbour, Violet
Carciente, Jacob. "Centenario de Nacimiento del Poeta Elias David Curiel," 352
———. *La Comunidad Judia de Venezuela 1610–1990,* 353
———. "Dispersion y unidad de la Nacion Judia," 245
———. "Los Judios de Barcelona (Venezuela)," 351

Cardoso, Izak Jesurun. *Three Centuries of Jewish Life in Curaçao,* **135**
Cardozo de Bethencourt, Louis. "Notes on the Spanish and Portuguese Jews in the United States, Guiana, and the Dutch and British West Indies," **18, 136, 205, 246, 303, 414, 486**
"Caribbean Diaspora." SEE Wilson, Samuel
Caribbeana. Containing Letters and Dissertations, **206**
Caribbeana — 1900–1965. SEE Comitas, Lambros
Carmichael, Gertrude. *The History of the West Indian Islands of Trinidad and Tobago,* **19, 446**
Carmoly, Eliakim. "La Famille Belinfante," **207**
———. "Les Israelites des deux Indes," **487**
Carvajal, Luis de. SEE Liebman, Seymour B., ed., *The Enlightened — The Writings of Luis de Carvajal,* **556**
Cassuto, Alfonso. "Items from the Old Minute Book of the Sephardic Congregation of Hamburg," **208**
Cavignac, Jean. *Dictionnaire du Judaisme Bordelais,* **415**
"Cayenne — A Chapter" (in Hebrew). SEE Loker, Zvi
"Centenario de Nacimiento del Poeta Elias David Curiel." SEE Carciente, Jacob
Centenario Kol Shearith Israel. SEE Melamed, Joseph, *1976, Centenario,* **388**
"The Chain" (in Hebrew). SEE Oliveira, Salomon ben David de

"Charles II and His Contract with Abraham Israel de Piso." SEE Oppenheim, Samuel
Chauleau, Liliane. "Tobago et la presence francaise," **20**
Chronological History. SEE Rodway, James, and Thomas Watt
"Chronological Sketch of the History of the Jews in Surinam." SEE Felsenthal, B., and Richard Gottheil
Chyet, Stanley F. *Lopez of Newport,* **488**
Chyet, Stanley F., ed. SEE Stiles, Ezra, *The Event is with the Lord,* **234a**
"Un cimetiere juif au Cap Haitien." SEE Loker, Zvi
Clayton Link. SEE Link, Marion Clayton
Clodore, Jean de. *Relation de ce qui s'est passe dans les Isles et Terre Ferme de l'Amerique,* **20a, 415a**
Le Code Noir. SEE Louis XIV, Roi de France et Navarre
"Code Noir." SEE Louis XIV, Roi de France et Navarre
Code of Laws for the Government of the Israelite Congregation in the Island of St. Thomas. SEE Nathan, M. N., E. C. Da Costa, and I. H. Osorio
Cohen, Mario E. *Bibliografia en idioma castellano del judaismo,* **490**
———. "Primeras sinagogas de America," **489**
Cohen, Martin A. "Religion of Luis Rodriguez Carvajal," **491**
Cohen, Robert. "Early Caribbean Jewry," **492**
———. *Jews in Another Environment, Surinam in the*

Second Half of the Eighteenth Century, 24
———. "A Mis-Dated Ketuba," 23
———. "New Aspects of the Egerton Manuscript," 21
———. "Passage to a New World: The Sephardi Poor of 18th Century Amsterdam," 22
Cohen, Robert, ed. *The Jewish Nation in Surinam*, 25
Cohen de Herrera, Avraham. "Gate of God" (in Hebrew), 493
Coke, Thomas. *A History of the West Indies*, 248, 494
Coleman, Edward D. "Bridgetown, Barbados," 209
The Colonial American Jew, 1492–1776. SEE Marcus, Jacob Rader
Colonial Coinage of the U.S. Virgin Islands. SEE Higgie, Lincoln W.
Colonising Expeditions to the West Indies and Guiana. SEE Harlow, V. T., ed.
Comitas, Lambros. *Caribbeana — 1900–1965*, 495
La Comunidad Hebrea de Panama, 378
La Comunidad Judia de Panama. SEE de Lima Jesurun, Hector
La Comunidad Judia de Venezuela 1610–1990. SEE Carciente, Jacob
"La communita Sefaradite di Recife e Curaçao." SEE Di Leone Leoni, Aron
Cone, G. Herbert. "Jews in Curaçao," 137
"Conflict and Opportunity." SEE Swetschinski, Daniel M.
Congregation Mikve Israel-Emanuel of Curaçao 1654. SEE Maslin, Simeon, *Guidebook*, 162

El Contrabando Holandes en el Caribe. SEE Arauz Monfante, Celestino Andres
"Contributions to the History of the Jews in Surinam," SEE Gottheil, Richard
"Conversos and Conversions in the Caribbean." SEE Loker, Zvi
Cooper, Leslie. *Rededication. Hebrew Congregation, Blessing and Peace*, 304
Corcos, Joseph M. *A Synopsis of the History of the Jews of Curaçao*, 138, 354
"Coro." SEE Rivero, Jose Felix
Corre, Alan. "Sephardim of the U.S.," 496
"Correspondence of the Mahamad." SEE Barnett, Richard
Cortissoz, S. "The Maduro Family," 497
Costa, Rini da. SEE Da Costa, Rini S. C.
Costa, S. C. da. SEE Da Costa, Rini S. C.
Coulthard, G. R. "Inscriptions on Jewish Gravestones in Jamaica," 249
Cramer, Jack. "Two Hemispheres and Centuries of History Buried in the Jewish Cemetery on Nevis," 305
"Cripto-Judios en Sao-Paulo." SEE Novinsky, Anita
Croitoru Rotbaum, Itic. *De Sefarad al Neosefardismo*, 355
Crouse, Nellis. *French Pioneers*, 417
———. *French Struggle for the West Indies 1665–1713*, **26**, 416

"Crypto Jews in Mexico during the seventeenth century." SEE Wiznitzer, Arnold

"Crypto Jews in Mexico during the sixteenth century." SEE Wiznitzer, Arnold

Cundall, Frank. "Press and Printers of Jamaica Prior to 1820," **250**

———. "The Taxation of Jews in Jamaica," **251**

———. "The Taxation of the Jews in Jamaica in the 17th Century," **252**

Cundall, Frank. SEE ALSO Davis, N. Darnell, Frank Cundall, and Albert M. Friedenberg

"Curaçao and Amsterdam Jewish Communities." SEE Kaplan, Yosef

[*Curaçao*]: *Willemstad, City of Monuments.* SEE Schwartz, Gary, *Willemstad*, **167**

D

Da Costa, E. C. SEE Nathan, M. N., E. C. Da Costa, and I. H. Osorio

Da Costa, Rini S. C. "De Gebeurtenissen in deze Eeuw op Jodensavanne," **30**

———. "De Geneeskrachtige Bron van de Joden Savanne," **28**

———. "Joden Savanne: een historische plaats in het oerwoud van Suriname," **29**

———. "De Kweekschool op de Joden Savanne," **27**

Daniel Levi de Barrios. SEE Pieterse, Wilhelmina Christina

Danish West Indies Under Company Rule. SEE Westergaard, Waldemar C.

"David de Is. C. Nassy, Author of the *Essai Historique sur Surinam.*" SEE Bijlsma, R.

"David D'Isaac Nassy." SEE Bloch, Harry

"David L. Yulee, Florida's First Senator." SEE Hühner, Leon

"David Nassy of Surinam." SEE Seeligmann, Sigmund

Davis, N. Darnell "Additional Notes on the History of the Jews of Barbados," **211**

———. "The Beginnings of British Guiana," **31**

———. "Notes from wills of the family of Massiah," **212**

———. "Notes on the History of the Jews of Barbados," **210**

Davis, David Brion. "Slave Trade and the Jews," **498**

Davis, N. Darnell, Frank Cundall, and **Albert M. Friedenberg.** "Documents Relating to the History of the Jews in Jamaica and Barbados," **213, 253**

D'Azevedo, João Lucio. SEE d'Azevedo, João Lucio

"Debate on Mr. Burke's motion relating to the . . . island of St. Eustatius," **175a**

De Curazao a Coro, la odisea de los Judios en Venezuela. SEE Delgado, Sonia

Deen, Lucille D. "Anglo-Dutch Relations from 1660 to 1688," **33**

De Groot, Silvia W. SEE Groot, Silvia W. de

Deive, Carlos Esteban. "Judios en Santo Domingo," **398**

de Laet. SEE Laet

Delgado, Sonia. *De Curazao a Coro, la odisea de los Judios en Venezuela,* **356**

De Lima, Arthur. *The De Limas of Frederick Street,* **447**

———. *The House of Jacob,* **448**

de Lima Jesurun, Hector. *La Comunidad Judia de Panama,* **379**

The De Limas of Frederick Street. SEE De Lima, Arthur

de Marchena Dujarric, Enrique. "Presencia hebrea en la Republica Dominicana," **399**

Dentz, Fred. Oudschans. SEE Oudschans Dentz, Fred.

de Oliveira. SEE Oliveira

DePass Scot, Rosemarie. "Spanish Portuguese Jews in Jamaica," **254**

de Pool, John. "Biografia de Dr Mordechai Ricardo," **141**

———. *El Primer chispazo de genio — Bolivar en Curaçao,* **139, 357**

———. *El primer chispazo de genio (una leyenda historica),* **140**

Description de la France Equinoctiale. SEE La Barre, Antoine Joseph Le Febvre de

Description Geographique de la Guyanne. SEE Bellin, Jacques Nicolas

Description of the Island of Jamaica. SEE Blome, Richard

De Sefarad al Neosefardismo. SEE Croitoru Rotbaum, Itic

de Sola Lazaron, Anita. *De Sola Odyssey,* **142**

De Sola Odyssey. SEE de Sola Lazaron, Anita

de Sola Pool, David. "The Burial Society of Curaçao in 1783," **143**

———. "Mohelim of Curaçao and Surinam," **36, 144, 501**

———. *Old Faith in the New World,* **503**

———. *Portraits Etched in Stone,* **502**

de Sola-Ricardo, Irma. "Juan de Sola," **358**

de Sousa, Ernest Henriquez. SEE Sousa, Ernest Henriquez de

Dicionario Biografico. SEE Wolff, Egon and Frieda

Dictionnaire du Judaisme Bordelais. SEE Cavignac, Jean

"Die or Leave: An Anti-Jewish Riot." SEE Aizenberg, Isidoro

Di Leone Leoni, Aron. "La communita Sefaradite di Recife e Curaçao," **176**

Dillen, J. G. van. "De Economische Positie en Betekenis der Joden," **504**

"La dispersion Crypto-Judia en Panama." SEE Osorio Osorio, Alberto

"Dispersion y unidad de la Nacion Judia." SEE Carciente, Jacob

Djudios de España i Portugal en la filatelia. SEE Arbell, Mordechai

"Dr. David Nassy in Surinam." SEE Gottheil, Richard

"Dr. S. de Jongh Ricardo." SEE Rivero, Jose Felix

"Documents Relating to the Attempted Departure of the Jews from Surinam 1675." SEE Hollander, J. H.

"Documents Relating to the History of the Jews in Jamaica and Barbados." SEE Davis, N. Darnell, Frank Cundall, and Albert M. Friedenberg

"Dona Sara de Coro, Venezuela." SEE Arbell, Mordechai

Dornsberg, Hendrick Willem, and **Cornelius Dornsberg.** *Beschrijving van de Plechtigheden nevens de Lofdichten en Gebeden, uitgesproken op het eerste Jubelfeest . . . op de Savane*, **37**.

"Dos Commerciantes Judios de la Epoca Colonial." SEE Aizenberg, Isidoro

Drie Eeuwen Jodendom in Suriname. SEE Morroy, Henk

Dulhuisen, Leo. SEE Bakker, Eveline, Leo Dulhuisen, and Mauritz Massankhan

Du Mount, Butel. SEE Butel-Dumont, Georges-Marie

Dunn, Richard S. "The Barbados Census of 1680," **214**

"Dutch Archives," SEE Bloom, Herbert I.

"The Dutch Caribbean and Its Metropolis." SEE Hoetink, H.

The Dutch in Brazil 1624–1654. SEE Boxer, Charles R.

The Dutch in the Caribbean and in the Guianas. SEE Goslinga, Cornelis Ch.

The Dutch in the Caribbean and on the Wild Coast. SEE Goslinga, Cornelis Ch.

"The Dutch in Western Guiana." SEE Edmonton, George

The Dutch Seaborne Empire. SEE Boxer, Charles R.

Dutertre, Jean Baptiste. *Histoire generale des Antilles Habitees par les Francois*, **37a, 417a**

E

"The Earliest Rabbis and Jewish Writers." SEE Kayserling, Meir

"Early Caribbean Jewry." SEE Cohen, Robert

"An Early Confirmation Certificate from the Island of St. Thomas." SEE Philipson, David

"Early French West Indian Records." SEE Ragatz, Lowell

"Early History of the Jews in New York." SEE Oppenheim, Samuel

"Early Jewish Colony in Western Guiana" (1907). SEE Oppenheim, Samuel

Early Jewish Colony in Western Guiana, 1658–1666. SEE Oppenheim, Samuel

"Early Jewish Colony in Western Guiana: supplemental data" (1909). SEE Oppenheim, Samuel

"Early Jewish Soldiers in London and Jamaica." SEE Kohler, Max

Early Jews of New Orleans. SEE Korn, Bertram Wallace

"Early Relations between American Jews and Eretz Yisrael." SEE Lehmann, Manfred R.

"Early Sephardic Jewish Settlers." SEE Fidanque, E. Alvin

Economic Activities of the Jews. SEE Bloom, Herbert I.

"De Economische Positie en Betekenis der Joden." SEE Dillen, J. G. van

Edmonton, George. "The Dutch in Western Guiana," **38**

"De eerste Jood op Curaçao." SEE Euwens, P. A.

Eight Chapters in the History of Jamaica. SEE Hill, Richard

"The 1855 Expulsion of the Curaçaoan Jews." SEE Aizenberg, Isidoro

"An Eighteenth-Century Plan to Invade Jamaica — Isaac

Yeshurun Sasportas." SEE Loker, Zvi
"An Eighteenth Century Prayer." SEE Loker, Zvi
Elias David Curiel. SEE Agudo Freites, Raul
Elkin, Judith Laikin. *Imagining Idolatry: Missionaries, Indians, and Jews,* **505**
Elmaleh, Leon H. *Jewish Cemetery,* **506**
Les Emissaires de la Terre Sainte. SEE Yaari, Abraham
Emmanuel, Isaac. "Fortunes and Misfortunes of the Jews in Brazil," **507**
———. "Jewish Education in Curaçao (1692–1802)," **145**
———. *Jews of Coro, Venezuela,* **359**
———. "Juifs de la Martinique et leur coreligionnaires," **418**
———. "El Portugues en la Sinagoga 'Mikve Israel' de Curaçao," **147**
———. *Precious Stones of the Jews of Curaçao,* **146**
———. "Seventeenth Century Brazilian Jewry," **508**
Emmanuel, Isaac and **Suzanne.** *History of the Jews of the Netherlands Antilles,* **148**
Emmanuel, Suzanne. SEE Emmanuel, Isaac and Suzanne
Enciclopedia Judaica Castellana, **509**
Encyclopaedia Judaica (Berlin, 1928), **510**
Encyclopaedia Sefardica Nederlandica, **511**
Encyclopedie van de Nederlandse Antillen, **512**
Encyclopedie van de Nederlandse West Indie, **513**
Encyclopedie van Suriname, **39**

English Colonies in Guiana and on the Amazon. SEE Williamson, James Alexander
The Enlightened — The Writings of Luis de Carvajal. SEE Liebman, Seymour B., ed.
"Een Episode uit de Joodsche Kolonisatie van Guyana 1660." SEE Zwarts, Jacob.
"Epitaphs in the Jewish Cemetery at Christianstad, St. Croix." SEE Heller, Bernard
Esbozo historico novelizado, y versos. SEE Levy Maduro, Emil
"Escritores Sefardies en Venezuela." SEE Molho, Isaac
Españoles sin patria y la raza sefardi. SEE Pulido Fernandez, Angel
Essai Historique sur la Colonie de Surinam. SEE Nassy, David de Isaac Cohen
Europe in the Caribbean. SEE Mitchell, Sir Harold
Euwens, P. A. "De eerste Jood op Curaçao," **149**
———. "De Joodsche Synagoge op Curaçao," **150**
Evans, Eli N. *Judah P. Benjamin — The Jewish Confederate,* **177, 306**
The Event is with the Lord. SEE Stiles, Ezra
"Excavation of Skeletal Material at Joden Savanne." SEE Khudabux, M. R.
"The Exodus from Brazil." SEE Wiznitzer, Arnold
"Exploring the Drowned City of Port Royal." SEE Link, Marion Clayton
"Expulsion of the Jews from Martinique." SEE Loker, Zvi
"Extract from an Old Document." SEE Oppenheim, Samuel

"Extractos y Comentarios del Almanaque." SEE Rojas Castro, Romulo

Ezratty, Harry A. "Komemorasion en Statia," **178**

———. "Old Sephardic Cemetery Reconsecrated in Nevis," **307**

———. "Statia," **179**

F

Faber, Eli. *A Time for Planting. The First Migration,* **514**

Fabius, G. J. "Het leenstelsel van de West Indische Compagnie," **40**

"The Failure of the Jewish Settlement in the Island of Tobago." SEE Arbell, Mordechai

La familia Fidanque. SEE Arjona, Nadhji

"Familia Herrera." SEE Perera, Ambrosio

"Die Familie Gradis." SEE Graetz, Heinrich

"La Famille Belinfante." SEE Carmoly, Eliakim

"Une famille juive au Cap — Membres de la famille Depas." SEE Loker, Zvi

"The Family of Gideon Abudiente." SEE Wolf, Lucien

"Family Structure and Jewish Continuity in Jamaica." SEE August, Thomas G.

Farah, Donna. "The Jewish Community in Trinidad," **449**

Farrar, P. A. "Jews in Barbados," **215**

Felice Cardot, Carlos. "Algunas acciones de los Holandeses en la region," **151, 359**

Felsenthal, B., and **Richard Gottheil.** "Chronological Sketch of the History of the Jews in Surinam," **41**

Ferro Tavares, Maria Jose Pimenta. *Os Judeus em Portugal,* **514a**

Fidanque, E. Alvin. "Early Sephardic Jewish Settlers," **515**

———. "Jews and Panama," **380**

———. *Jews and Panama,* **381**

Fidanque, E. Alvin, et al. *Kol Shearith Israel — Cien Anos,* **382**

Fidanque Family. SEE Arjona, Nadhji, *La familia Fidanque,* **377**

Fidanque Levy, Emma. *Fidanques in the Western Hemisphere,* **384**

———. "Fidanques: Symbols of the Continuity," **383**

"The Fidanques, Hidalgos of Faith." SEE Salomon, H. P.

"Fidanques: Symbols of the Continuity." SEE Fidanque Levy, Emma

Fidelity, Faith, Freedom: the Fidanques in the Western Hemisphere. SEE Fidanque Levy, Emma

Finkel, Haim. "Two Ancient Maps Illustrating the Early History of the Jews of Surinam," **42**

The First Colonization of Tobago by the Courlanders and the Dutch. SEE Goslinga, Cornelis Ch.

"First Sephardic Cemeteries." SEE Böhm, Günter

"First Settling of Jews in Surinam." SEE Gompers, Joseph

Fontaine, Jos. *Uit Suriname's Historie,* **43**

"Forgotten Jews Who Saved the American Revolution." SEE Lehmann, Manfred R.

Fortique, Jose Rafael. *Los Motines Anti-Judios de Coro,* **361**
———. "Los sucesos de 1831 contra los judios de Coro," **362**
Fortune, Stephen A. *Merchants and Jews,* **216, 255, 516**
"Fortunes and Misfortunes of the Jews in Brazil." SEE Emmanuel, Isaac
Franco Mendes, David. "History of the Late Haham" (in Hebrew), **517**
French Pioneers. SEE Crouse, Nellis
French Struggle for the West Indies 1665–1713. SEE Crouse, Nellis
Frere, George. *Short History of Barbados,* **217**
Friede, Juan, ed. *Gonzalo Jimenez de Quesada,* **363**
Friedenberg, Albert M. SEE Davis, N. Darnell, Frank Cundall, and Albert M. Friedenberg
Friedenwald, Herbert. "Material for the History of the Jews in the West Indies," **256**
Friedman, Lee M. "Gabriel Milan, the Jewish Governor of St. Thomas," **309**
———. "Joshua Montefiore of St. Albans, Vermont," **218**
———. *Rabbi Haim Isaac Carigal,* **518**
———. "Some References to Jews in the 'Sugar Trade'," **519**
———. "Wills of Early Settlers in New York," **308**
La fusion de los Sefardies con los Dominicanos. SEE Ucko, Enrique

G

"Gabriel Milan og somme af hans samtid." SEE Krarup, Frederik
"Gabriel Milan, the Jewish Governor of St. Thomas." SEE Friedman, Lee M.
Gans, Mozes Heiman. *Memorbook,* **520**
Garrett, Hester. *Gravestone Inscriptions — St. Eustatius,* **180**
Gaspar da Gama. SEE Lipiner, Elias
Gastmann, Albert. *Historical Dictionary,* **521**
"Gate of God" (in Hebrew). SEE Cohen de Herrera, Avraham
"De Gebeurtenissen in deze Eeuw op Jodensavanne." SEE Da Costa, Rini S. C.
"Genealogical Note." SEE Maduro, M. L.
"Genealogical Resources." SEE Bennett, Ralph G.
"De Geneeskrachtige Bron van de Joden Savanne." SEE Da Costa, Rini S. C.
Geneology of the Belinfante Family. SEE Belinfante, Frederik Jozef
A General Description of the West-Indian Islands. SEE Singleton, John
"The genesis and the exodus, life and death of Jews on St. Eustatius." SEE Strouse, Samuel S.
Gerbier, Balthazar. *Sommary Description,* **522**
"Die Geschichte der Niederlassung der Juden in Holland." SEE Sommerhausen, H.
Geschiedenis van de Kolonien Essequebo, Demerary en Berbice. SEE Netscher, Pieter Martinus
Geschiedenis van Suriname (1861). SEE Wolbers, J.

Geschiedenis van Suriname (1993). See Bakker, Eveline, Leo Dulhuisen, and Mauritz Massankhan

Geschiedkundige tijdtafel van Suriname. See Bueno de Mesquita, J. A., and Fred. Oudschans Dentz

Global Culture, Island Identity — Continuity and Change in the Afro-Caribbean Community of Nevis. SEE Olwig, Karen Fog

Gompers, Joseph. "First Settling of Jews in Surinam," **44**

Gonsalves de Mello, Jose Antonio. "A Nacao Judaica do Brasil Holandes," **523**

———. "Primera comunidad Judia," **524**

Gonzalo Jimenez de Quesada. SEE Friede, Juan, ed.

Goodwin, R. Christopher. *Survey of Honen Dalim, St. Eustatius,* **181**

Gordon, Joyce. *Nevis, Queen of the Caribees,* **310**

Goslinga, Cornelis Ch. *The Dutch in the Caribbean and in the Guianas,* **528**

———. *The Dutch in the Caribbean and on the Wild Coast,* **525**

———. *The First Colonization of Tobago by the Courlanders and the Dutch,* **45**

———. "De Nederlandse Antillen en Suriname," **527**

———. *Short History of the Netherlands Antilles and Surinam,* **526**

Gottheil, Richard. "Contributions to the History of the Jews in Surinam," **46**

———. "Dr. David Nassy in Surinam," **47**

Gottheil, Richard. SEE ALSO Felsenthal, B., and Richard Gottheil

"Governor Mauricius." SEE Meiden, G. W. van der

Graetz, Heinrich. "Die Familie Gradis," **419**

The Grandees. SEE Birmingham, Stephen

Gravestone Inscriptions — St. Eustatius. SEE Garrett, Hester

Groot, Silvia W. de. "Pierre Jacques Benoit in Surinam," **47a**

———. "Summary with Annotations," **47b**

Grunwald, Max. *Portugiesengräber auf deutscher Erde,* **219**

Guiana. SEE Rodway, James

Guidebook: The Historic Synagogue of . . . Congregation Mikve Israel-Emanuel. SEE Maslin, Simeon J.

Guterman, Vida Lindo. SEE Lindo Guterman, Vida

H

"Haham de Cordova of Jamaica." SEE Korn, Bertram W.

Hacohen, Yosef. "A History" (in Hebrew), **529**

Hamelberg, J. H. J. *De Nederlanders op de West-Indische Eilanden,* **152, 182, 530**

———. *Tobago. Een vergeten Nederlandsche Kolonie,* **48**

Harlow, V. T. *A History of Barbados, 1625–1685,* **220**

Harlow, V. T., ed. *Colonising Expeditions to the West Indies and Guiana,* **49, 531**

Hartog, J. *History of St. Eustatius,* **184**

———. "The Honen Dalim Congregation," **183**

———. *The Jews and St. Eustatius,* 185

———. "Jose Diaz Pimienta," 532

Hartsinck, Jan Jacob. *Beschryving van Guiana of de Wilde Kust in Zuid-America,* 50

Hayne, Samuel. *Abstract of all the Statutes made concerning aliens,* 221

"Hebrew Loyalty." SEE Abrahams, I.

Heller, Bernard. "Epitaphs in the Jewish Cemetery at Christianstad, St. Croix," 312

Henriques, Fernando. *Jamaica, Land of Wood and Water,* 257

Henriques, S. Q., "Special Taxation of the Jews," 533

Hickeringill, Capt. Edmund. *Jamaica Viewed,* 258

Hilfman, P. A. "Notes on the History of the Jews in Surinam, 51

Higgie, Lincoln W. *Colonial Coinage of the U.S. Virgin Islands,* 313

Hill, Richard. *Eight Chapters in the History of Jamaica,* 259

Hiss, Philip Hanson. *Netherlands America,* 534

"Une Histoire de la Litterature Juive de Daniel Levi de Barrios." SEE Kayserling, Meir

Histoire des Antilles. SEE Pluchon, Pierre, ed.

L'Histoire du Nouveau Monde. SEE Laet, Joannes de

Histoire et commerce des Antilles Angloises. SEE Butel-Dumont, Georges-Marie

Histoire Generale des Antilles Habitees par les Francois. SEE Dutertre, Jean Baptiste

Historia de la Ciudad de David. SEE Osorio Osorio, Alberto

"Historia de la Familia Lopez Penha." SEE Lopez Penha, Moises

"Historia de la familia Lopez-Penha 1660–1924." SEE Arbell, Mordechai

Historia de los Portugueses en Venezuela. SEE Acosta Saignes, Miguel

Historia dos Cristãos Novos. SEE d'Azevedo, João Lucio

Historical and Chronological Deduction. SEE Anderson, Adam

Historical Dictionary. SEE Gastmann, Albert

Historical essay. SEE Nassy, David de Isaac Cohen

Historie en Oude families van de Nederlandse Antillen. SEE Krafft, A. J. C.

Historische Proeve over de Kolonie Suriname. SEE Samson, Ph. A.

"A History" (in Hebrew). SEE Hacohen, Yosef

History of Barbados. SEE Schomburgk, Sir Robert H.

History of Barbados: from Amerindian Settlement to Nation-State. SEE Beckles, Hilary

History of Barbados, 1625–1685. SEE Harlow, V. T.

History of Jamaica. SEE Long, Edward

History of St. Eustatius. SEE Hartog, J.

History of the British West Indies. SEE Burns, Sir Alan.

History of the Jews in America. SEE Wiernik, Peter

"History of the Jews of America" (in Hebrew). SEE Razin, Mordecai Zeev

"History of the Jews of Jamaica." SEE Judah, George Fortunatus

History of the Jews of the Netherlands Antilles. SEE Emmanuel, Isaac and Suzanne

"History of the Late Haham" (in Hebrew). SEE Franco Mendes, David

A History of the Marranos. SEE Roth, Cecil

History of the West Indian Islands of Trinidad and Tobago. See Carmichael, Gertrude

History of the West Indies. SEE Coke, Thomas

History of Tobago. SEE Woodcock, Henry Iles

Hodges, William. *Juifs au Cap,* **420**

Hoetink, H. "The Dutch Caribbean and Its Metropolis," **52, 153**

———. *El Pueblo Dominicano,* **400**

Hoetink, H., ed. SEE *Encyclopedie van de Nederlandse Antillen,* **512**

Hollander, J. H. "Documents Relating to the Attempted Departure of the Jews from Surinam 1675," **53**

Holzberg, Carol S. *Minorities and Power in a Black Society: The Jewish Community of Jamaica,* **260**

"Homenaje a Don Jacobo Jose Curiel." SEE Zubillaga Perera, Cecilio

"The Honen Dalim Congregation." SEE Hartog, J.

Honoring 1776 and Famous Jews, **536**

Hooker, Bernard. *United Congregation Shaare Shalom, Kingston,* **261**

The House of Jacob. SEE De Lima, Arthur

Hubbard, Vincent K. "Synagogue Rediscovered," **314**

Hühner, Leon. "David L. Yulee, Florida's First Senator," **315**

———. "Whence Came the First Jewish Settlers," **537**

Huisman, Piet. *Sephardim: the spirit,* **154**

"Hunt's Bay Jewish Cemetery, Kingston, Jamaica." SEE Silverman, Henry Phillips

Hurwitz, Edith. SEE Hurwitz, Samuel and Edith

Hurwitz, Samuel and **Edith.** *Jamaica, A Historical Portrait,* **263**

———. "The New World Sets an Example for the Old: The Jews of Jamaica and Political Rights, 1661–1831," **262**

Hyamson, Albert M. *Sephardim of England,* **538**

I

Imagining Idolatry: Missionaries, Indians and Jews. SEE Elkin, Judith Laikin

"La independencia de Venezuela y los judios." SEE Nassi, Mario

The Inquisitors and the Jews of the New World. SEE Liebman, Seymour B.

"Inscriptions Juives dans les cimetieres." SEE Arbell, Mordechai

"Inscriptions on Jewish Gravestones in Jamaica." SEE Coulthard, G. R.

Interesting tracts, relating to the Island of Jamaica, **264**

"Introduction to Early American Jewish History" (in Hebrew). SEE Marcus, Jacob Rader

"Inventaire des Biens d'Isaac Henriquez Moron." SEE Loker, Zvi

"Isac de Castro." SEE Wiznitzer, Arnold

"Isaac Yeshurun Sasportas — French Patriot or Jewish Radical Idealist?" SEE Loker, Zvi, "An Eighteenth-Century Plan . . . ," **275**

Israel, Herbert. "Wandering in the Caribbean Area," **539**

"Les Israelites des deux Indes." SEE Carmoly, Eliakim

"La Istoria de los Sefardis en las Islas de Martinique, Guadeloupe." SEE Arbell, Mordechai

"Items from the Old Minute Book of the Sephardic Congregation of Hamburg." SEE Cassuto, Alfonso

"Items Relating to the History of the Jews." SEE Phillips, N. Taylor

Izaque de Castro. SEE Lipiner, Elias

J

Jamaica, A Historical Portrait. SEE Hurwitz, Samuel and Edith

Jamaica, Land of Wood and Water. SEE Henriques, Fernando

Jamaica Viewed. SEE Hickeringill, Capt. Edmund

Janin, Joseph. *Religion aux colonies francaises,* **421**

Jaramillo Levi, Enrique. "La Saga de la Familia Osorio," **385**

Jenkinson, Sir Anthony. "St. Paul's Church Tower in Port Royal," **265**

"Jerusalem aan de Suriname rivier. Pioniers hunkerend naar Heilige Land." SEE Arbell, Mordechai and Barouh Lionarons

Jesurun, Hector de Lima. SEE de Lima

"Jewish Assimilation and the Plural Society in Jamaica." SEE August, Thomas

Jewish Calendar. SEE Lindo, Elias Hiam

Jewish Cemetery. SEE Elmaleh, Leon H.

"The Jewish Cemetery at Charlestown, Nevis." SEE Oliver, Vere Langford

"The Jewish Community in Surinam." SEE Lier, Rudolf van

"The Jewish Community in Trinidad." SEE Farah, Donna

"Jewish Community of St. Eustatius" (Hebrew). SEE Arbell, Mordechai

"Jewish Customs among the Suriname . . . Population." SEE Oppenheim, J. D.

"Jewish Education in Curaçao (1692–1802)." SEE Emmanuel, Isaac

The Jewish Encyclopedia, **540**

"Jewish Epitaphs in the West Indies, St. Thomas." SEE Wilhelm, Kurt

Jewish Historical Development in the Virgin Islands. SEE Paiewonsky, Isidor

The Jewish Nation in Surinam. SEE Cohen, Robert, ed.

Jewish Pioneers in America. SEE Lebeson, Anita Libman

The Jewish Question. SEE Blyden, Edward

"Jewish Settlement in the West Indies." SEE Sonne, Isaiah

"Jewish Studies in Dutch Brazil." SEE Wiznitzer, Arnold

"The Jewish Synagogue." SEE Shilstone, E. M.

Jewish Tombstone Inscriptions. SEE Wright, Philip

"Jews and Panama." SEE Fidanque, E. Alvin

Jews and Panama. SEE Fidanque, E. Alvin

The Jews and St. Eustatius. SEE Hartog, J.

"Jews and the Guianas." SEE Roth, Cecil

Jews in Another Environment, Surinam in the Second Half of the Eighteenth Century. SEE Cohen, Robert

"Jews in Barbados." SEE Farrar, P. A.

"Jews in Barbados in 1739." SEE Oppenheim, Samuel

Jews in Colonial Brazil. SEE Wiznitzer, Arnold

"Jews in Curaçao." SEE Cone, G. Herbert

"Jews in Jamaica and Daniel Israel Lopez Laguna." SEE Kayserling, Meir

"Jews in Surinam." SEE Summit, Alphons

Jews in the Caribbean. SEE Loker, Zvi

"Jews in the Grand'Anse." SEE Loker, Zvi

Jews of Coro, Venezuela. SEE Emmanuel, Isaac S.

"Jews of Exotic Surinam and Their History." See Bennett, Ralph G.

"Jews of Jamaica. A Historical View." SEE Schlesinger, Benjamin

"The Jews of Jamaica and Political Rights, 1661–1831," SEE Hurwitz, Samuel and Edith, "The New World Sets an Example for the Old," **262**

"Jews of Jamaica and St Michael." SEE Roth, Cecil

"The Jews of Nevis." SEE Marsden-Smedley, Hester

"Jews of Speightown — Barbados." SEE Stoute, Edward

"Jews of the Caribbean." SEE Wigoder, Geoffrey

"Jews of the Virgin Islands. SEE Alland, Alexander

"Jews of Tudor England." SEE Wolf, Lucien

"Jews' Tribute in Jamaica." SEE Judah, George Fortunatus

"Joden in Suriname." SEE Regeling, D.

"Joden Savanne: een historische plaats in het oerwoud van Suriname." SEE Da Costa, Rini S. C.

"Joden-Savanne in Suriname." SEE Kopuit, M.

Johnson, Eugene. "Sephardim of Jamaica," **266**

"De Joodsche Synagoge op Curaçao." SEE Euwens, P. A.

"Joodse Kleuringen." SEE Oudschans Dentz, Fred.

"Jose Diaz Pimienta." SEE Hartog, J.

"Joshua Montefiore of St. Albans, Vermont." SEE Friedman, Lee M.

"Joshua Piza and His Descendants." SEE Lindo Guterman, Vida

Journal of a Lady of Quality. SEE Schaw, Janet

Journal of her Residence in Jamaica from 1801 to 1805. SEE Nugent, Lady Maria

Journals of the Assembly of Jamaica (Kingston), **267**

Journey through Suriname. (P. J. Benoit). SEE Groot, Sylvia W. de, "Summary with Annotations," **47b**

"Juan de Sola." SEE de Sola-Ricardo, Irma

"Juan de Ylan." SEE Loker, Zvi

Judah, George Fortunatus. "History of the Jews of Jamaica," **268**

———. "Jews' Tribute in Jamaica," **269**

"Judah P. Benjamin as a Jew." SEE Korn, Bertram W.

"Judah P. Benjamin — Statesman and Jurist." SEE Kohler, Max

Judah P. Benjamin — The Jewish Confederate. SEE Evans, Eli N.

"Judaismo de los Cristianos nuevos." SEE Uchmany, Eva Alexandra

Judaismo e Inquisicion en Panama. SEE Osorio Osorio, Alberto

"Juden in Surinam." SEE Kayserling, Meir

"Judeus de Surinam." SEE d'Azevedo, Joao Lucio

Os Judeus em Portugal. SEE Ferro Tavares, Maria Jose Pimenta

Judeus, Judaizantes e seus Escravos. SEE Wolff, Egon and Frieda

Judeus no Brasil Imperial. SEE Wolff, Egon and Frieda

El Judio en Costa Rica. SEE Schifter, Jacobo

Judios Conversos. SEE Saban, Mario Javier

"Los Judios de Barcelona (Venezuela)." SEE Carciente, Jacob

"Los Judios de San Eustaquio" (1976). SEE Liebman, Seymour B.

"Los Judios de San Eustatius" (1987). SEE Liebman, Seymour B.

"Judios en la Caracas del 1800." SEE Aizenberg, Isidoro

"Los judios en la epoca colonial." SEE Mesa Bernal, Daniel

Los Judios en Mexico y America Central. SEE Liebman, Seymour B.

"Judios en Santo Domingo." SEE Deive, Carlos Esteban

"Judios Hispano Portugueses del Caribe." SEE Arbell, Mordechai

"Los Judios y la opinion publica en el Brasil." SEE Teensma, Benjamin

"Juif portugais: fondateur de Moron?" SEE Loker, Zvi

"Les Juifs a Cayenne." SEE Loker, Zvi

"Les Juifs a la Martinique." SEE Petitjean-Roget, J.

Juifs au Cap. SEE Hodges, William

"Juifs dans les colonies francaises." SEE Cahen, Abraham

"Juifs dans les Colonies hollandaises." SEE Kohut, George Alexander

"Juifs de la Martinique." SEE Cahen, Abraham

"Juifs de la Martinique et leur coreligionnaires." SEE Emmanuel, Isaac

"Juifs de Saint-Eustache." SEE Plot, Serge

Les Juifs d'Espagne. SEE Mechoulan, Henry, directeur

"Juifs et Protestants aux Antilles Francaises." SEE Rennard, Jules

"Jungle Jews." SEE Vandercook, John Womack

K

Kalina. SEE Pisk, Rosita Kalina de

Kaplan, Yosef. "Curaçao and Amsterdam Jewish Communities," **155**

———. "The Reencounter with Judaism" (in Hebrew), **541**

Karner, Frances P. *The Sephardics of Curaçao,* **156**

Kayserling, Meir. "The Earliest Rabbis and Jewish Writers," **542**

———. "Une Histoire de la Litterature Juive de Daniel Levi de Barrios," **543**

———. "Jews in Jamaica and Daniel Israel Lopez Laguna," **270**

———. "Juden in Surinam," **54**

Kesler, C. K. "Tobago. Een vergeten Nederlandsche Kolonie," **55**

Khudabux, M. R. "Excavation of Skeletal Material at Joden Savanne," **56**

Kisch, Hyman J. "Los memorables sefaraditas de la Republica Dominicana," **401**

Kleyntjens, J. "De Koerlandse Kolonisatiepogingen op Tobago," **57**

Klopmann, Ewald von. "Abrege de l'histoire de Tobago," **58**

Koeman, C., ed., et al., *Links with the Past,* **59**

"De Koerlandse Kolonisatiepogingen op Tobago." SEE Kleyntjens, J.

Kohler, Max J. "Early Jewish Soldiers in London and Jamaica," **271**

———. "Judah P. Benjamin — Statesman and Jurist," **316**

———. "Some Early American Zionist Projects," **544**

Kohut, George Alexander. "Juifs dans les Colonies hollandaises," **186**

———. "Sketches of Jewish loyalty, bravery and patriotism," **545**

———. "Who Was the First Rabbi of Surinam?" **60**

De Kolonisatie van de Portugeesch Joodsche Natie. SEE Oudschans Dentz, Fred.

"De kolonisatie van Guiana." SEE Oudschans Dentz, Fred.

Kol Shearith Israel — Cien Anos. SEE Fidanque, E. Alvin, et al.

"Komemorasion en Statia." SEE Ezratty, Harry A.

Kopuit, M. "Joden-Savanne in Suriname," **61**

Korn, Bertram Wallace. *American Jewry: the Formative Years.* SEE HIS "The Period of Growth of Power"

———. *Early Jews of New Orleans,* **546**

———. "Haham de Cordova of Jamaica," **272**

———. "Judah P. Benjamin as a Jew," **317**

———. "The Period of Growth of Power" (in Hebrew), **547**
Krafft, A. J. C. *Historie en Oude families van de Nederlandse Antillen,* **157**
Krarup, Frederik. "Gabriel Milan og somme af hans samtid," **317a**
Krohn, Franklin B. "Search for the Elusive Caribbean Jews," **548**
"De Kweekschool op de Joden Savanne," SEE Da Costa, Rini S. C.
"De Kweekschool op de Joden Savanne." SEE Samson, Ph. A.

L

La Barre, Antoine Joseph Le Febvre de. *Description de la France Equinoctiale,* **61a, 421a**
Labat, Jean Baptiste. *Nouveau Voyage,* **62, 422**
———. *Nuevo Viaje,* **423**
———. *Voyage du Chevalier,* **63**
Laet, Joannes de. *L'Histoire du Nouveau Monde,* **549**
De Landbouw in de Kolonie Suriname. SEE Teenstra, Marten D.
Larsen, Jens. *Virgin Islands Story,* **318**
Lazaron, Anita de Sola. SEE de Sola Lazaron, Anita
Lebeson, Anita Libman. *Jewish Pioneers in America,* **550**
"Het leenstelsel van de West Indische Compagnie." SEE Fabius, G. J.
Le Febvre de La Barre. SEE La Barre
Lehmann, Manfred R. "Early Relations between American Jews and Eretz Yisrael," **222, 551**
———. "Forgotten Jews Who Saved the American Revolution," **187**
———. "Pre-Nuptial Agreements in Colonial Days," **273**
———. "Prominent Religious Leaders in the Joden Savanna," **65**
———. "Some Tombstones from the Joden Savanna," **64**
———. "Visit to Surinam" (Hebrew), **66**
Leistenschneider, Maria. "Presidente Juan Lindo," **386**
Leonard, Robert. "The Maduro Family and Their Tokens," **552**
"Letter of David Nassy." SEE Oppenheim, Samuel
"Letters and Dissertations." SEE *Caribbeana*
Levi de Barrios, Daniel. "Triumphal carro de la Perfeccion," **67**
Levy, B. H. *Savannah's Old Jewish Community Cemeteries,* **553**
Levy, Emma Fidanque. SEE Fidanque Levy, Emma
Levy Maduro, Emil. *Esbozo historico novelizado, y versos,* **364**
Lewin, Boleslao. "Los Portugueses en Buenos Aires," **554**
Lewisohn, Florence, "Alexander Hamilton's West Indian Boyhood," **319**
Lichtveld, Lou. *A Valuable document concerning Tobago — 1647,* **69**
Liebman, Seymour B. *The Inquisitors and the Jews of the New World,* **558**
———. "Los Judios de San Eustaquio" (1976), **188**

———. "Los Judios de San Eustatius" (1987), **189**
———. *Los Judios en Mexico y America Central*, **557**
———. *New World Jewry*, **560**
———. "Religion y costumbres judias," **562**
———. *Requiem por los olvidados*, **561**
———. "Research Problems in Mexican Jewish History," **555**
———. "Secret Jewry," **563**
———. "Tomas Trevino de Sobremonte," **559**
Liebman, Seymour B., ed. *The Enlightened — The Writings of Luis de Carvajal*, **556**
Lier, Rudolf van. "The Jewish Community in Surinam," **69b**
———. *Samenleving in een grensgebied*, **69a**
Ligon, Richard. *A True & Exact History of the Island of Barbados*, **223**
Lima Jesurun, Hector de. SEE de Lima
Lindo, Alicia. "Sketch of the Life of David Lindo," **274**
Lindo, Elias Hiam. *Jewish Calendar*, **564**
Lindo Guterman, Vida. "Joshua Piza and His Descendants," **565**
Link, Marion Clayton. "Exploring the Drowned City of Port Royal," **274a**
Link, Pablo. *Aporte Judio al descubrimiento*, **566**
Links with the Past. SEE Koeman, C., ed.
Lionarons, Barouh. SEE Arbell, Mordechai, and Barouh Lionarons
Lipiner, Elias. *Gaspar da Gama*, **567**

———. *Izaque de Castro*, **568**
"List of Jews Made Denizens." SEE Oppenheim, Samuel
"List of Properties Situated in Saint Domingue," SEE Archives Nationales, Paris
"List of Wills in the West Indies Institute, Kingston." SEE Wilson, Dorit
"List of Wills of Jews." SEE Oppenheim, Samuel
List of Works . . . Relating to . . . Jews in Various Countries. SEE New York Public Library
Lockward, Alfonso. "Presencia Judia en Santo Domingo," **402**
Lockward, Alfonso, ed. *Presencia Judia en Santo Domingo*, **403**
Loix et Constitutions. SEE Moreau de Saint-Mery, Mederic Louis Elie
Loker, Zvi. "Cayenne — A Chapter" (in Hebrew), **71**
———. "Un cimetiere juif au Cap Haitien," **427**
———. "Conversos and Conversions in the Caribbean," **570**
———. "An Eighteenth-Century Plan to Invade Jamaica — Isaac Yeshurun Sasportas — French Patriot or Jewish Radical Idealist?" **275**
———. "An Eighteenth Century Prayer," **70**
———. "Expulsion of the Jews from Martinique," **433**
———. "Une famille juive au cap: Membres de la famille Depas," **425**
———. "Inventaire des Biens d'Isaac Henriquez Moron," **431**
———. *Jews in the Caribbean*, **569**

130

———. "Jews in the Grand'Anse," **430**
———. "Juan de Ylan," **158**
———. "Un Juif portugais: fondateur de Moron?" **428**
———. "Les Juifs a Cayenne," **72**
———. "Lopez de Paz," **424**
———. "On the Jewish Colony at Remire," **73**
———. "Simon Isaac Henriquez Moron," **429**
———. "Toponymies juives en Haiti," **426**
———. "Were there Jewish Communities in Saint Domingue (Haiti)?" **432**
London Times Editor. *Refutation of various calumnies.* SEE West India Proprietor
Long, Edward. *History of Jamaica,* **277**
Loor, A. H. SEE Koeman, C., ed., **59**
"Lopez de Paz." SEE Loker, Zvi
Lopez of Newport. SEE Chyet, Stanley F.
Lopez Penha, Moises. "Historia de la Familia Lopez Penha," **571**
Lopez Ruiz, Juvenal. "El Universo Poetico de Elias David Curiel," **365**
Louis XIV, Roi de France et Navarre. *Le Code Noir,* **434**
———. "Code Noir," **435**
"The Lucas Manuscript Volumes in the Barbados Public Library," **224**
"Lucien Wolf en de Joodsche Kolonisatie." SEE Oudschans Dentz, Fred.
The Lying Hero. SEE Mathews, Samuel Augustus

M

Macpherson, David. *Annals of Commerce,* **572**
Maduro, Antonio J. *Spaanse documenten uit de Jaren 1639 en 1640,* **159**
Maduro, Emil L. SEE Levy Maduro, Emil
Maduro, M. L. "Genealogical Note," **160**
Maduro, Rene. *Our Snoa ... Synagogue Mikve Israel,* **161**
"The Maduro Family." SEE Cortissoz, S.
"The Maduro Family and Their Tokens." SEE Leonard, Robert
Manco Bermudez, Dino. SEE Bermudez, Dino Manco
"Manner in which Believers in the Mosaic Faith." SEE Bille, Frants Ernest
Marcus, Jacob Rader. *American Jewry: Documents,* **575**
———. *The Colonial American Jew 1492–1776,* **278**
———. "Introduction to Early American Jewish History" (in Hebrew), **576**
———. Review of *The Sephardim of England* by Albert M. Hyamson, **574**
———. "West India and South America Expedition," **573**
Margolinsky, Jul. "298 Epitaphs from the Jewish Cemetery in St. Thomas," **320**
Marsden-Smedley, Hester. "The Jews of Nevis," **321**
Maslin, Simeon J. *Guidebook: The Historic Synagogue of Congregation Mikve Israel-Emmanuel of Curaçao,* **162**

———. "1732 and 1982 in Curaçao," **163**

———. "Toward the Preservation of Caribbean Jewish Monuments," **577**

Massankhan, Mauritz. SEE Bakker, Eveline, Leo Dulhuisen, and Mauritz Massankhan

"Material for the History of the Jews in the West Indies." SEE Friedenwald, Herbert

Mathews, Samuel Augustus. *The Lying Hero*, **578**

"Max Delvalle Henriques," **387**

Mechoulan, Henry, directeur. *Les Juifs d'Espagne*, **579**

Meijer, J. *M. J. Lewenstein's Opperrabinaat te Paramaribo 1857–1864*, **76**

———. *Pioneers of Pauroma*, **74**

———. *Van Corantijn tot Marowijne*, **75**

Meiden, G. W. van der. "Governor Mauricius," **73a**

Melamed, Joseph. *1976, Centenario Kol Shearith Israel*, **388**

Mello, Jose Antonio Gonsalves de. SEE Gonsalves de Mello, Jose Antonio

"Members of the Brazilian Jewish Community." SEE Wiznitzer, Arnold

"Membres de la famille Depas." SEE Loker, Zvi, "Une famille juive au cap," **425**

"Los memorables sefaraditas de la Republica Dominicana." SEE Kisch, Hyman J.

Memorbook. SEE Gans, Mozes Heiman

Mendes, David Franco. SEE Franco Mendes, David

Mendes, H. P. "Privileges Granted by the British Government, **77**

Mendes Chumaceiro, Ronald. "Mendes Chumaceiro Family," **580**

"Mendes Chumaceiro Family." SEE Mendes Chumaceiro, Ronald

Menkman, W. R. "Suriname in Willoughby's Tijd," **78**

Merchants and Jews. SEE Fortune, Stephen A.

Merchants Map. SEE Roberts, Lewes

"Merchants of Bordeaux." SEE Webster, Jonathan H.

Merrill, Gordon. "Role of the Sephardic Jews," **581**

Mesa Bernal, Daniel. "Los judios en la epoca colonial," **365**

Metropoles et peripheries Sefarades d'Occident. SEE Nahon, Gerard

Metz, Allan. "'Those of the Hebrew Nation . . .'," **582**

Minorities and Power in a Black Society: The Jewish Community of Jamaica. SEE Holzberg, Carol S.

"Minute Book of Congregations." SEE Wiznitzer, Arnold

Mirelman, Victor A. "Sephardim in Latin America," **583**

"The Misdated Ketuba." SEE Cohen, Robert

Mitchell, Sir Harold. *Europe in the Caribbean*, **584**

Mitrasingh, Benjamin S. "Archeological Investigation at Joden Savanne," **79**

M. J. Lewenstein's Opperrabinaat te Paramaribo 1857–1864. SEE Meijer, J.

Author/Title Index

Mogollon, Juan Angel. "El Poeta Elias David Curiel," **367**
"Mohelim of Curaçao and Surinam." SEE de Sola Pool, David
Molho, Isaac. "Escritores Sefardies en Venezuela, **368**
———. "El poeta y dramaturgo Michael de Barrios," **80**
Molho, Yitzhak. SEE Molho, Isaac
Monumental Inscriptions in the Burial Ground of the Jewish Synagogue at Bridgetown. SEE Shilstone, E. M.
Monumental Inscriptions in the Churches and Churchyards. SEE Oliver, Vere Langford
Monumental Inscriptions of the British West Indies. SEE Oliver, Vere Langford
Moore, Brian. "Race, Power and Social Segmentation," **81**
"Mordehay Ricardo en Timbro." SEE Arbell, Mordechai
Moreau de Saint-Mery, Mederic Louis Elie. *Loix et Constitutions,* **436**
Morroy, Henk. *Drie Eeuwen Jodendom in Suriname,* **82**
Los Motines Anti-Judios de Coro. SEE Fortique, Jose Rafael
du Mount, Butel. SEE Butel-Dumont, Georges-Marie

N

"A Nacao Judaica do Brasil Holandes." SEE Gonsalves de Mello, Jose Antonio
"A Nacao Judaica Portuguesa do Surinam a e sua relacoes com o Brazil no seculo XVIII." See Barata, Mario

"*La Nacion.*" SEE Arbell, Mordechai
"La 'Nacion Judia'." SEE Arbell, Mordechai
Nahon, Gerard. *Metropoles et peripheries Sefarades d'Occident,* **587**
———. *Les "Nations" Juives Portugaises du Sud-Ouest,* **83**
———. "Relations entre Amsterdam et Constantinople," **586**
———. "Une source pour l'histoire de la diaspora Sefarade," **585**
"The Name of the Country Surinam." SEE Oudschans Dentz, Fred.
"Names on Stones in Savan Cemetery, Charlotte Amalie." SEE Robles, Jacob
Narrative, of a Five Years' Expedition. SEE Stedman, John Gabriel
Nassi, David. SEE Nassy, David de Isaac Cohen
Nassi, Mario. "La independencia de Venezuela y los judios," **369**
"De Nassi's in Suriname." SEE Soestadijk, S. Kalb
Nassy, David de Isaac Cohen. *Essai historique sur la colonie de Surinam,* **84**
———. *Historical essay on the colony of Surinam,* **84a**
Nathan, M. N., E. C. Da Costa, and I. H. Osorio. *Code of Laws for the Government of the Israelite Congregation in the Island of St. Thomas,* **322**
Les "Nations" Juives Portugaises du Sud-Ouest. SEE Nahon, Gerard

De Nederlanders op de West-Indische Eilanden. SEE Hamelberg, J. H. J.

"De Nederlandse Antillen en Suriname." SEE Goslinga, Cornelis Ch.

Nelemans, B. SEE Koeman, C., ed.

Netherlands America. SEE Hiss, Philip Hanson

Netscher, Pieter Martinus. *Geschiedenis van de Kolonien Essequebo, Demerary en Berbice,* **85**

Nevis, Queen of the Caribees. SEE Gordon, Joyce

"New Aspects of the Egerton Manuscript." SEE Cohen, Robert

Newman, Aubrey. "Sephardim of the Caribbean," **588**

New World Jewry. SEE Liebman, Seymour B.

"The New World Sets an Example for the Old: The Jews of Jamaica and Political Rights, 1661–1831," SEE Samuel and Edith Hurwitz

New York Public Library. "List of works . . . relating to . . . Jews in various countries," **589**

Nieuhof, Johan. "Voyages and Travels into Brasil," **590**

"1992: 500 Years after Columbus." SEE Arbell, Mordechai

1976: Centenario Kol Shearith Israel. SEE Melamed, Joseph

No peace beyond the line. SEE Bridenbaugh, Carl and Roberta

"Notas sobre o judaismo e a Inquisicao." SEE d'Azevedo, João Lucio

"Note on the Jewish Community of St. Thomas." SEE Campbell, Albert A.

"Notes from wills of the family of Massiah." SEE Davis, N. Darnell

"Notes on the Follow-up of the Jews of Recife." SEE Stern, Malcolm H.

"Notes on the History of the Jews of Barbados." SEE Davis, N. Darnell

"Notes on the History of the Jews in Surinam. See Hilfman, P. A.

"Notes on the Jews' Tribute in Jamaica." SEE Rosenbloom, Joseph R.

"Notes on the Spanish and Portuguese Jews in the United States, Guiana, and the Dutch and British West Indies." SEE Cardozo de Bethencourt, Louis

Notice Historique sur la Guyane Francaise. SEE Ternaux-Compans, Henri

Nouveau Voyage. SEE Labat, Jean Baptiste

Nouvelles Frances. SEE Boucher, Philip P.

Novinsky, Anita. "Cripto-Judios en Sao-Paulo," **592**

———. "Sefardies en Brazil colonial," **593**

———. "Sephardim in Brazil," **591**

Nuestras Gentes. SEE Bermudez, Dino Manco, and Jose Watnik Baron

Nuevo Viaje. SEE Labat, Jean Baptiste

Nuevos antecedentes. SEE Böhm, Günter

Nugent, Lady Maria. *Journal of her Residence in Jamaica from 1801 to 1805,* **280**

O

A Odisseia dos Judeus de Recife. SEE Wolff, Egon and Frieda

Old Faith in the New World. SEE de Sola Pool, David

"Old Sephardic Cemetery Reconsecrated in Nevis." SEE Ezratty, Harry A.

Oliveira, Salomon ben David de. "The Chain" (in Hebrew), **594**

Oliver, Vere Langford. "The Jewish Cemetery at Charlestown, Nevis," **323**

———. *Monumental Inscriptions in the Churches and Churchyards,* **226**

———. *Monumental Inscriptions of the British West Indies,* **595**

Oliveyra, Solomon ben David de. SEE Oliveira

Olwig, Karen Fog. *Global Culture, Island Identity — Continuity and Change in the Afro-Caribbean Community of Nevis,* **324**

"On the Jewish Colony at Remire." SEE Loker, Zvi

Oostindie, Gert. "Synagogen aan de Wilde Kust," **86**

Oppenheim, J. D. "Jewish Customs among the Suriname ... Population," **87**

Oppenheim, Samuel. "Charles II and His Contract with Abraham Israel de Piso," **281**

———. "Early History of the Jews in New York," **596**

———. "Early Jewish Colony in Western Guiana" (1907), **88**

———. *Early Jewish Colony in Western Guiana, 1658–1666,* **89**

———. "Early Jewish Colony in Western Guiana: supplemental data" (1909), **90**

———. "Extract from an Old Document," **228**

———. "Jews in Barbados in 1739," **227**

———. "Letter of David Nassy," **91**

———. "List of Jews Made Denizens," **597**

———. "List of Wills of Jews," **598**

Origin of Commerce. SEE Anderson, Adam, *Historical ... Deduction,* **452**

Osorio, I. H. SEE Nathan, M. N., E. C. Da Costa, and I. H. Osorio

Osorio Osorio, Alberto. "La dispersion Crypto-Judia en Panama," **391**

———. *Historia de la Ciudad de David,* **389**

———. *Judaismo e Inquisicion en Panama,* **390**

———. *Los Osorios Sefardies,* **392**

Los Osorios Sefardies. SEE Osorio Osorio, Alberto

Oudschans Dentz, Fred. "Joodse Kleuringen," **94**

———. *De Kolonisatie van de Portugeesch Joodsche Natie,* **91a**

———. "De kolonisatie van Guiana," **92**

———. "Lucien Wolf en de Joodsche Kolonisatie," **599**

———. "The Name of the Country Surinam," **95**

———. "Wat er overbleef van het Kerkhof" (1948), **93**

———. "Wat er overbleef van het Kerkhof" (1962), **96**

Oudschans Dentz, Fred. SEE ALSO Bueno de Mesquita, J. A., and Fred. Oudschans Dentz
Our Snoa . . . Synagogue Mikve Israel. SEE Maduro, Rene
An Outline of Barbados History. SEE Campbell, P. F.

P

Paiewonsky, Isidor. "Camille Pissarro, St. Thomas," **326**
———. *Jewish Historical Development in the Virgin Islands,* **325**
Panorama of Jamaica Jewry. SEE Silverman, Henry Phillips
Pares, Richard. *War and Trade in the West Indies,* **600**
———. *A West-India Fortune,* **327**
———. *Yankees and Creoles,* **601**
Parliamentary History of England. SEE "Debate on Mr. Burke's Motion"
Parry, J. H., Philip Sherlock, and Anthony Maingot. *A Short History of the West Indies,* **602**
Participation Judia. SEE Rosenthal, Ludwig
"Passage to a New World: The Sephardi Poor of 18th Century Amsterdam." SEE Cohen, Robert
Peller, Aaron. *United Netherlands Portuguese Congregation,* **164**
Perera, Ambrosio. "Familia Herrera," **370**
Perera, Cecilio Zubillaga. SEE Zubillaga Perera, Cecilio
"The Period of Growth of Power" (in Hebrew). SEE Korn, Bertram Wallace
Petitjean-Roget, J. "Les Juifs a la Martinique," **437**

Philipson, David. "An Early Confirmation Certificate from the Island of St. Thomas," **328**
Phillips, N. Taylor. "Items Relating to the History of the Jews of New York," **603**
Philosophical and Political History of the Settlements and Trade. SEE Raynal, Abbe
Pictorial Featuring Some Aspects of Jamaica's Jewry. SEE Sousa, Ernest Henriquez de
"Pierre Jacques Benoit in Surinam," SEE Groot, Silvia W. de
Pieterse, Wilhelmina Christina. *Daniel Levi de Barrios,* **98**
Pimenta Ferro Tavares, Maria Jose. SEE Ferro Tavares, Maria Jose Pimenta
Pioneers of Pauroma. SEE Meijer, J.
Pisk, Rosita Kalina de. "Sefaraditas en Costa Rica, **393**
Pissarro, **329**
Plot, Serge. "Juifs de Saint-Eustache," **191**
Pluchon, Pierre, ed. *Histoire des Antilles,* **99, 438**
"El Poeta Elias David Curiel." SEE Mogollon, Juan Angel
"El poeta y dramaturgo Michael de Barrios." SEE Molho, Isaac
Pool, David de Sola. SEE de Sola Pool, David
Pool, John de. SEE de Pool, John
Portraits Etched in Stone. SEE de Sola Pool, David
Portugiesengräber auf deutscher Erde. SEE Grunwald, Max
"El Portugues en la Sinagoga 'Mikve Israel' de Curaçao." SEE Emmanuel, Isaac

Author/Title Index

"Portuguese Sephardim." SEE Stern, Malcolm H.
"Los Portugueses en Buenos Aires." SEE Lewin, Boleslao
Postal, Bernard. SEE Stern, Malcolm, and Bernard Postal
Precious Stones of the Jews of Curaçao. SEE Emmanuel, Isaac
"Pre-Nuptial Agreements in Colonial Days." SEE Lehmann, Manfred R.
"Presencia hebrea en la Republica Dominicana." SEE de Marchena Dujarric, Enrique
"Presencia Judia en Santo Domingo." SEE Lockward, Alfonso
Presencia Judia en Santo Domingo. SEE Lockward, Alfonso, ed.
"The Preservation of the Sephardic Records of the Island of St. Thomas, Virgin Islands." SEE Baa, Enid M.
"Presidente Juan Lindo." SEE Leistenschneider, Maria
"Press and Printers of Jamaica Prior to 1820." SEE Cundall, Frank
"The Press in British Guiana." SEE Rodway, James
El Primer chispazo de genio — Bolivar en Curaçao. SEE de Pool, John
El primer chispazo de genio (una leyenda historica). SEE de Pool, John
"Primera comunidad Judia." SEE Gonsalves de Mello, Jose Antonio
"Primeras sinagogas de America." SEE Cohen, Mario E.
"Las Primeras sinagogas Sefaradies." SEE Böhm, Günter

"Privateers and Pirates." SEE Barbour, Violet
"Privileges Granted by the British Government. SEE Mendes, H. P.
"Prominent Religious Leaders in the Joden Savanne." SEE Lehmann, Manfred R.
"The Provenance of the First Jews in New Amsterdam." SEE Wolff, Egon and Frieda
Publicacao e provizional reglamento de Sua Alteza. SEE Willem Carel Hendrik Friso, Prince of Orange and Nassau
El Pueblo Dominicano. SEE Hoetink, H.
Pulido Fernandez, Angel. *Españoles sin patria y la raza sefardi,* **605**

Q

"Quakers, Jews and Freedom of Teaching." SEE Cadbury, Henry J.
Quantos Judeus. SEE Wolff, Egon and Frieda

R

Rabbi Haim Isaac Carigal. SEE Friedman, Lee M.
"Race, Power and Social Segmentation." SEE Moore, Brian
Ragatz, Lowell. "Early French West Indian Records," **439**
"Raices Centenares del Pueblo Hebreo en la Republica de Panama." SEE Arjona, Nadhji
"Rapport van de Colonie Essequibo en Demerary," **99a**
"Rapport van het Eiland Curaçao," **164a**

Raynal, Abbe. *Philosophical and Political History of the Settlements and Trade,* **606**

Razin, Mordecai Zeev. "History of the Jews of America" (in Hebrew), **607**

A Record of the Jews in Jamaica. SEE Andrade, Jacob A. P. M.

"Records of a West Indian Mohel," **282**

Records of the Earliest Jewish Community. SEE Wiznitzer, Arnold

Rededication. Hebrew Congregation, Blessing and Peace. SEE Cooper, Leslie

"The Reencounter with Judaism" (in Hebrew). SEE Kaplan, Josef

A refutation of various calumnies against the West India Colonies. SEE West India Proprietor

Regeling, D. "Joden in Suriname," **100**

Reglamento Consernente a Nacao Judaica. SEE Willem Carel Hendrik Friso, Prince of Orange and Nassau

Reize naar Surinamen. SEE Stedman, John Gabriel

Relation de ce qui s'est passe dans les Isles et Terre Ferme de l'Amerique. SEE Clodore, Jean de

Relation de la prise des Isles de Goree au Cap-Vert et de Tabago, **100a**

"Relations entre Amsterdam et Constantinople." SEE Nahon, Gerard

Religion aux colonies francaises. SEE Janin, Joseph

"Religion of Luis Rodriguez Carvajal." SEE Cohen, Martin A.

"Religion y costumbres judias." SEE Liebman, Seymour B.

Relkin, Stanley T., and Monty R. Abrams. *A Short History of the Hebrew Congregation of St. Thomas,* **330**

Rennard, Jules. "Juifs et Protestants aux Antilles Francaises," **440**

Rens, L. L. E. "Analysis of Annals Relating to the Early Jewish Settlement," **101**

"Report on Journey to Belize City, Belize — Visit to the Jewish Burial Ground." SEE Ainbinder, Pierre

Report on the Sir John Vaughan Papers. SEE Vosper, Edna

Requiem por los olvidados. SEE Liebman, Seymour B.

"Research Problems in Mexican Jewish History." SEE Liebman, Seymour B.

"Response of the Knowledgeable" (in Hebrew). SEE Ben-Yitzhak, Yohanan

Review of *Minorities and Power in a Black Society* by Carol S. Holzberg. SEE August, Thomas

Review of *Precious Stones of Curaçao* by Isaac Emmanuel. SEE Stern, Malcolm H.

"Review of the Jewish Colonists in Barbados 1680." SEE Samuel, Wilfred S.

Review of *The Sephardim of England* by Albert M. Hyamson. SEE Marcus, Jacob Rader

Revolution dans Saint Domingue. SEE Brutus, Edner

Rivero, Jose Felix. "Coro," **372**

———. "Dr. S. de Jongh Ricardo," **371**

Author/Title Index

Rivkind, Isaac. "Some Remarks about Messengers from Palestine to America," **608**

Roberts, Lewes. *Merchants Map*, **102**

Robles, Jacob. "Names on Stones in Savan Cemetery, Charlotte Amalie," **332**

———. "St. Thomas Burials 1792–1802," **331**

———. "St. Thomas Confirmations 1843–1934," **333**

Rochefort, Charles de. *Le Tableau de l'isle de Tobago*, **103**

Rodway, James. *Guiana*, **104**

———. "The Press in British Guiana," **105**

———. *West Indies and the Spanish Main*, **192, 609**

Rodway, James, and Thomas Watt. *Chronological History*, **106**

Rojas Castro, Romulo. "Extractos y Comentarios del Almanaque," **165**

"Role of the Sephardic Jews." SEE Merrill, Gordon

Roos, J. S. "Additional Notes on the History of the Jews of Surinam," **107**

Rosenbloom, Joseph R. "Notes on the Jews' Tribute in Jamaica," **283**

Rosenthal, Ludwig. *La Participation Judia*, **610**

Roth, Cecil. *A History of the Marranos*, **611**

———. "Jews and the Guianas," **108**

———. "Jews of Jamaica and St Michael," **284**

S

Saban, Mario Javier. *Judios Conversos*, **612**

"La Saga de la Familia Osorio." SEE Jaramillo Levi, Enrique

"St. Eustatius," **193**

St. Eustatius, Historical Gem of the Caribbean. SEE Attema, Yipie

St. Juste, L'Aurore. "Ancestres Pierre Mendes-France," **441**

"St. Paul's Church Tower in Port Royal." SEE Jenkinson, Sir Anthony

"St. Thomas Burials 1792–1802." SEE Robles, Jacob

"St. Thomas Confirmations 1843–1934." SEE Robles, Jacob

Salomon, H. P. "The Fidanques, Hidalgos of Faith," **394**

Samenleving in een grensgebied. SEE Lier, Rudolf van

Samson, Ph. A. *Historische Proeve over de Kolonie Suriname*, **109**

———. "De Kweekschool op de Joden Savanne," **111**

———. "Voorrechten aan de Joden in Suriname Verleend," **110**

Samuel, Wilfred S. "Review of the Jewish Colonists in Barbados 1680," **230**

———. "Will of Rabbi Carigal," **229**

Saruco, Jahacob de Selomoh Hisquiau. SEE Bassan, Abraham Jehisquia, *Sermoes funebres*, **468**

Savannah's Old Jewish Community Cemeteries. SEE Levy, B. H.

Schachner, Nathan. *Alexander Hamilton*, **334**

Schaw, Janet. *Journal of a Lady of Quality*, **193a**

Schifter, Jacobo. *El Judio en Costa Rica,* **395**

Schilder, G. SEE Koeman, C., ed.

Schlesinger, Benjamin. "Jews of Jamaica. A Historical View," **285**

Schomburgk, Sir Robert H. *The History of Barbados,* **232**

Schopflocher, Roberto. "Vigencia de la Inquisicion," **613**

Schwartz, Gary. *Willemstad, City of Monuments,* **167**

"Search for the Elusive Caribbean Jews." SEE Krohn, Franklin B.

"Secreete Memorie," **111a**

"Secret Jewry." SEE Liebman, Seymour B.

Seeligmann, Sigmund. "David Nassy of Surinam," **112**

"Sefaradis de Pauroma." SEE Arbell, Mordechai

"Sefaradis i el dezvelopamiento ... de Sud-Amerika," SEE Arbell, Mordechai

"Sefaraditas en Costa Rica." SEE Pisk, Rosita Kalina de

"Sefardies en Brazil colonial." SEE Novinsky, Anita

Sefardies en los dominios holandeses. SEE Böhm, Günter

Sephardi Heritage. SEE Barnett, Richard

Sephardi Itinerary 1992. SEE Brenner, Frederic

"Sephardic Communities in the Virgin Islands." SEE Baa, Enid M.

"The Sephardic Diaspora" (in Hebrew). SEE Wigoder, Geoffrey

The Sephardics of Curaçao. SEE Karner, Frances P.

"Sephardim in Brazil." SEE Novinsky, Anita

"Sephardim in Latin America." SEE Mirelman, Victor A.

Sephardim of England. SEE Hyamson, Albert M.

"Sephardim of Jamaica." SEE Johnson, Eugene

"Sephardim of the Caribbean." SEE Newman, Aubrey

"Sephardim of the U.S." SEE Corre, Alan

Sephardim: the spirit. SEE Huisman, Piet

Sermoes Funebres. SEE Bassan, Abraham Jehisquia

"1732 and 1982 in Curaçao." SEE Maslin, Simeon J.

"Seventeenth Century Brazilian Jewry." SEE Emmanuel, Isaac

The Seventh Birthday Party. SEE Camps-Campins, Adrian

The Seventy-Fifth Anniversary of the Founding of the Synagogue Shaare Shalom. SEE Silverman, Henry Phillips

Shabethai, Haim. "Study of Life" (in Hebrew), **614**

Shilstone, E. M. "The Jewish Synagogue," **234**

———. *Monumental Inscriptions in the Burial Ground of the Jewish Synagogue at Bridgetown,* **233**

Short History of Barbados. SEE Frere, George

A Short History of the Hebrew Congregation of St. Thomas. SEE Relkin, Stanley T., and Monty R. Abrams

Short History of the Netherlands Antilles and Surinam. SEE Goslinga, Cornelis Ch.

A Short History of the West Indies. SEE Parry, J. H., Philip Sherlock, and Anthony Maingot

Sijpesteijn. SEE Sypesteyn
Silverman, Henry Phillips.
"Hunt's Bay Jewish Cemetery, Kingston, Jamaica," **286**
———. *Panorama of Jamaica Jewry* (alternate title), **287, 288**
———. *The Seventy-Fifth Anniversary of the Founding of the Synagogue Shaare Shalom,* **288**
———. *Tercentenary of the Official Founding of the Jewish Community of Jamaica 1655–1955,* **287**
"Simon Isaac Henriquez Moron." SEE Loker, Zvi
Singleton, John. *A General Description of the West-Indian Islands,* **194**
"Sketch of the Life of David Lindo." SEE Lindo, Alicia
"Sketches of Jewish loyalty, bravery and patriotism." SEE Kohut, George Alexander
"Slave Trade and the Jews." SEE Davis, David Brion
Sloane, Hans. *Voyage to the Islands Madera, Barbados, Nieves, S. Christophers and Jamaica,* **289**
"Social control in the Preemancipation Society of Kingston." SEE Bailey, Wilma R.
Soestadijk, S. Kalb. "De Nassi's in Suriname," **113**
Sola. SEE de Sola
"Some Aspects of the Early Jewish Community on the Island of St. Eustatius." SEE Strouse, Samuel S.
"Some Early American Zionist Projects." SEE Kohler, Max J.
"Some Notes on the Jews of Nevis." SEE Stern, Malcolm H.

"Some References to Jews in the 'Sugar Trade'." SEE Friedman, Lee M.
"Some Remarks about Messengers from Palestine to America." SEE Rivkind, Isaac
"Some Tombstones from the Joden Savanne." SEE Lehmann, Manfred R.
Sommary Description. SEE Gerbier, Balthazar
Sommerhausen, H. "Die Geschichte der Niederlassung der Juden in Holland," **615**
Sonne, Isaiah. "Jewish Settlement in the West Indies," **616**
"Une source pour l'histoire de la diaspora Sefarade." SEE Nahon, Gerard
Sousa, Ernest Henriquez de *Pictorial Featuring Some Aspects of Jamaica's Jewry,* **290**
Spaanse documenten uit de Jaren 1639 en 1640. SEE Maduro, Antonio J.
"Spanish Jews, a story" (in Hebrew). SEE Arbell, Mordechai
"Spanish Portuguese Jews in Jamaica." SEE DePass Scot, Rosemarie
Special Hymns of Temple Kahal Kados Yangakob, **396**
"Special Taxation of the Jews." SEE Henriques, S. Q.
"Statia." SEE Ezratty, Harry A.
Stedman, John Gabriel. *Narrative, of a Five Years' Expedition Against the Revolted Negroes,* **114**
———. *Reize naar Surinamen,* **115**
Stern, Malcolm H. *Americans of Jewish Descent,* **617**

———. "Notes on the Follow-up of the Jews of Recife," **619**

———. "Portuguese Sephardim," **618**

———. Review of *Precious Stones of Curaçao* by Isaac Emmanuel, **168**

———. "Some Notes on the Jews of Nevis," **335**

———. "Successful Caribbean Restoration, The Nevis Story," **336**

Stern, Malcolm, and Bernard Postal. *American Airlines Tourist's Guide to Jewish History in the Caribbean,* **620**

"De stichting van de Portugeesch-Joodsche gemeente en Synagoge in Suriname." SEE Bijlsma, R.

Stiles, Ezra. *The Event is with the Lord,* **234a**

"Stones of Memory. Revelations from a Cemetery." SEE Weinstein, Rochelle

Stoute, Edward. "Jews of Speightown — Barbados," **235**

Strouse, Samuel S. "The genesis and the exodus, life and death of Jews on St. Eustatius," **195**

———. "Some Aspects of the Early Jewish Community on the Island of St. Eustatius," **196**

"A Study of Brazilian Jewish History." SEE Bloom, Herbert I.

"Study of Life" (in Hebrew). SEE Shabethai, Haim

"A Study of the Life of the Jews in Jamaica as Reflected in Their Wills 1692–1798." SEE Zielonka, David M.

"Successful Caribbean Restoration, The Nevis Story." SEE Stern, Malcolm H.

"Los sucesos de 1831 contra los judios de Coro." SEE Fortique, Jose Rafael

Summary Description. SEE Gerbier, Balthazar, *Sommary Description,* **522**

"Summary with Annotations." SEE Groot, Silvia W. de

Summit, Alphons. "Jews in Surinam," **116**

"Suriname in Willoughby's Tijd." SEE Menkman, W. R.

Survey of Honen Dalim, St. Eustatius. SEE Goodwin, R. Christopher

Swetschinski, Daniel M.
"Conflict and Opportunity," **621**

"Synagogen aan de Wilde Kust." SEE Oostindie, Gert

"Synagogue and Cemetery of the Jewish Community in Recife." SEE Wiznitzer, Arnold

"Synagogue Rediscovered." SEE Hubbard, Vincent K.

"Synagogues of Surinam." SEE Böhm, Günter

A Synopsis of the History of the Jews of Curaçao. SEE Corcos, Joseph M.

Sypesteyn, C. A. van. *Beschrijving van Suriname,* **116a**

T

Table of Contents and biographical Index to Andrade's A Record of the Jews in Jamaica. SEE White, Paul F.

Le Tableau de L'isle de Tobago. SEE Rochefort, Charles de

"The Taxation of Jews in Jamaica." SEE Cundall, Frank

Author/Title Index

"The Taxation of the Jews in Jamaica in the 17th Century." SEE Cundall, Frank

Teensma, Benjamin. "Los Judios y la opinion publica en el Brasil," **622**

Teenstra, Marten D. *De Landbouw in de Kolonie Suriname,* **117**

Temminck Groll, C. L., and A. R. H. Tjin a Djie. *Architektuur van Suriname,* **118**

Tercentenary of the Official Founding of the Jewish Community of Jamaica 1655–1955. SEE Silverman, Henry Phillips

Ternaux-Compans, Henri. *Notice Historique sur la Guyane Francaise,* **119**

du Tertre, R. P. SEE Dutertre, Jean Baptiste

"'Those of the Hebrew Nation . . .'." SEE Metz, Allan

Three Centuries of Jewish Life in Curaçao. SEE Cardoso, Izak Jesurun

A Time for Planting. The First Migration. SEE Faber, Eli

Tjin a Djie, A. R. H. SEE Temminck Groll, C. L., and A. R. H. Tjin a Djie

Tobago. Een vergeten Nederlandsche Kolonie. SEE Hamelberg. J. H. J.

"Tobago. Een vergeten Nederlandsche Kolonie." SEE Kesler, C. K.

"Tobago et la presence francaise." See Chauleau, Liliane

"Tomas Trevino de Sobremonte." SEE Liebman, Seymour B.

"Tombstones in Barbados." SEE Barnett, R. D.

"Toponymies juives en Haiti." SEE Loker, Zvi

Tourist's Guide to Jewish History in the Caribbean. SEE Stern, Malcolm, and Bernard Postal, *American Airlines Tourist's Guide,* **620**

"Toward the Preservation of Caribbean Jewish Monuments." SEE Maslin, Simeon J.

"Triumphal carro de la Perfeccion." SEE Levi de Barrios, Daniel

A True & Exact History of the Island of Barbados. SEE Ligon, Richard

"Two Ancient Maps Illustrating the Early History of the Jews of Surinam." SEE Finkel, Haim

"Two Hemispheres and Centuries of History Buried in the Jewish Cemetery on Nevis." SEE Cramer, Jack

"298 Epitaphs from the Jewish Cemetery in St. Thomas." SEE Margolinsky, Jul.

U

Uchmany, Eva Alexandra. "El Judaismo de los Cristianos nuevos," **623**

Ucko, Enrique. *La Fusion de los Sefardies con los Dominicanos,* **404**

Uit Suriname's Historie. SEE Fontaine, Jos

United Congregation Shaare Shalom, Kingston. SEE Hooker, Bernard

United Netherlands Portuguese Congregation. SEE Peller, Aaron

"El Universo Poetico de Elias David Curiel." SEE Lopez Ruiz, Juvenal

V

A Valuable document concerning Tobago — 1647. SEE Lichtveld, Lou

Van Corantijn tot Marowijne. SEE Meijer, J.

Vandercook, John Womack. "Jungle Jews," **121**

Van der Meiden. SEE Meiden, W. van der

Van Lier. SEE Lier, Rudolf van

Van Punt en Snoa. SEE Buddingh', Bernard R.

Van Sijpesteijn. SEE Sypesteyn, C. A. van

"Venezuela y los Judios Venezuelanos." SEE Aizenberg, Isidoro

"Vida Judia en Chile y en Peru." SEE Böhm, Günter

"Vigencia de la Inquisicion." SEE Schopflocher, Roberto

Virgin Islands Story. SEE Larsen, Jens

"Visit to Surinam" (Hebrew). SEE Lehmann, Manfred R.

"Voorrechten aan de Joden in Suriname Verleend." SEE Samson, Ph. A.

Vosper, Edna. *Report on the Sir John Vaughan Papers,* **197**

Voyage de la France equinoxiale en l'isle de Cayenne entrepris par les Francois en l'annee M.DC.LII. SEE Biet, Antoine

Voyage du Chevalier. SEE Labat, Jean Baptiste

A Voyage to the Demerary. SEE Bolingbroke, Henry

Voyage to the Islands Madera, Barbados, Nieves, S. Christophers and Jamaica. SEE Sloane, Hans

"Voyages and Travels into Brasil." SEE Nieuhof, Johan

W

"Wandering in the Caribbean Area." SEE Israel, Herbert

War and Trade in the West Indies. SEE Pares, Richard

"Wat er overbleef van het Kerkhof" (1948 & 1962). SEE Oudschans Dentz, Fred.

Watnik Baron, Jose. SEE Bermudez, Dino Manco, and Jose Watnik Baron

Watt, Thomas. SEE Rodway, James, and Thomas Watt

Webster, Jonathan H. "Merchants of Bordeaux," **443**

Weinstein, Rochelle. "Stones of Memory. Revelations from a Cemetery," **169**

Wekker, J. B. Ch. SEE Koeman, C., ed.

"Were there Jewish Communities in Saint Domingue (Haiti)?" SEE Loker, Zvi

Westergaard, Waldemar C. *Danish West Indies Under Company Rule,* **337**

"West India and South America Expedition." SEE Marcus, Jacob Rader

A West-India Fortune. SEE Pares, Richard

West India Proprietor. *A refutation of various calumnies against the West India Colonies,* **290a**

West Indies and the Spanish Main. SEE Rodway, James

"Whence Came the First Jewish Settlers." SEE Hühner, Leon

Author/Title Index

White, Paul F. *Table of Contents and Biographical Index to Andrade's A Record of the Jews in Jamaica,* **291**

"Who Was the First Rabbi of Surinam?" SEE Kohut, George Alexander

Wiernik, Peter. *History of the Jews in America,* **624**

Wigoder, Geoffrey. "Jews of the Caribbean," **625**

———. "The Sephardic Diaspora" (in Hebrew), **626**

Wilhelm, Kurt. "Jewish Epitaphs in the West Indies, St. Thomas," **338**

"Will of Rabbi Carigal." SEE Samuel, Wilfrid S.

Willem Carel Hendrik Friso, Prince of Orange and Nassau. *Publicacao e provizional reglamento de Sua Alteza,* **169a**

———. *Reglamento Consernente a Nacao Judaica,* **170**

Willemstad, City of Monuments. SEE Schwartz, Gary

William IV, Prince of Orange. SEE Willem Carel Hendrik Friso, Prince of Orange and Nassau

Williamson, James A. *English Colonies in Guiana and on the Amazon 1604–1668,* **126**

"Wills of Early Settlers in New York." SEE Friedman, Lee M.

Wilson, Dorit. "List of Wills in the West Indies Institute, Kingston," **292**

Wilson, Samuel. "Caribbean Diaspora," **627**

Wiznitzer, Arnold. "Crypto Jews in Mexico during the seventeenth century," **637**

———. "Crypto Jews in Mexico during the sixteenth century," **636**

———. "The Exodus from Brazil and Arrival in New Amsterdam," **631**

———. "Isac de Castro," **634**

———. "Jewish Studies in Dutch Brazil, 1630–1654" **633**

———. *Jews in Colonial Brazil,* **635**

———. "The Members of the Brazilian Jewish Community," **629**

———. "The Minute Book of Congregations," **628**

———. *The Records of the Earliest Jewish Community in the New World,* **630**

———. "The Synagogue and Cemetery of the Jewish Community in Recife," **632**

Wolbers, J. *Geschiedenis van Suriname,* **127**

Wolf, Lucien. "American Elements in the Resettlement," **128, 638**

———. "The Family of Gideon Abudiente," **236, 339**

———. "Jews of Tudor England," **639**

Wolff, Egon and **Frieda.** *Dicionario Biografico,* **643**

———. *Judeus, Judaizantes e seus Escravos,* **644**

———. *Judeus no Brasil Imperial,* **641**

———. *A Odisseia dos Judeus de Recife,* **642**

———. "The Provenance of the First Jews in New Amsterdam," **640**

———. *Quantos Judeus,* **645**

Wolff, Frieda. SEE Wolff, Egon and Frieda
Woodcock, Henry Iles. *A History of Tobago,* **129**
Wright, Philip. *Jewish Tombstone Inscriptions,* **293**
The Writings of Luis de Carvajal El Mozo. SEE Liebman, Seymour B.

Y

Yaari, Abraham. *Les Emissaires de la Terre Sainte,* **646**
Yankees and Creoles. SEE Pares, Richard
Yerushalmi, Hayim Yosef. "Between Amsterdam and New Amsterdam," **171**

Z

Zager, Melvin R. "Aspects of the Economic, Religious and Social History of the 18th Century Jamaican Jews Derived from Their Wills," **294**
Zielonka, David M. "A Study of the Life of the Jews in Jamaica as Reflected in Their Wills 1692–1798," **295**
Zubillaga Perera, Cecilio. "Homenaje a Don Jacobo Jose Curiel," **373**
Zwarts, Jacob. "Een Episode uit de Joodsche Kolonisatie van Guyana 1660," **132**

Index of Subjects

A

Aboab. *See* Abohav
Abohav da Fonseca, R. Isaac, 493
Abudiente. *See* Obediente
administrators, Jewish, in Trinidad, 444, 446
advertisement, to attract planters to the Caribbean, 522
agriculture
  Jews in agro-industries, 2
  Jews in Guiana, 108
Aguilar, Moshe Rafael, 517
Alvares Correa (family), 452
American Jewish Archives, expedition to Caribbean and Guianas, 573
American Jews, 535, 576, 607
  relations with the Holy Land, 222
American Revolution, St. Eustatius Jews' role in, 187, 188, 189
Amsterdam, 201, 397, 474, 571, 581
  commerce with Dutch American colonies, 464
  relations between Jewish community of Curaçao and Jewish community of, 155
  relations between Jews in and Martinique Jews, 418
anti-Semitism, in Coro, 362
archeology
  excavations in Nevis, 314
  research in Jewish Savanne, 56, 79
architecture, Surinam, 118
archives, 573
  Amsterdam, 132, 508, 586
  American Jewish history and Dutch, 472
  Dutch Brazil Jews, 628
  French National, 439
  Jewish records in Charlotte Amalie, 297
  New York State material on Jews in Curaçao, 137
  West India Company, 90
Ashkenazi Jewish community, Suriname, 76
Athias, R. David Israel, 468

B

Barbados, history of, 200, 204, 220, 223, 232
  Jews in, 210, 211, 213, 214
Barrios, Daniel Levi de. *See* Levi de Barrios, Daniel
Barrios, J. H. de, Jr., 84
Barrios, Miguel. *See* Levi de Barrios, Daniel
Belinfante (fam.), 201, 207
Benjamin, Judah P., 177, 316, 317
Benoit, Pierre Jacques, 47a, 47b

Beraka ve Shalom synagogue (Suriname), 37
Berbice River, settlements on, 16
Bevis Marks Synagogue, 466
bibliography, 589
    on Caribbean, 495
    French colonial activities, 410
    Jews and conversos in Spanish colonial America, 490
"Black Code," text of, 434, 435
blacks, 94, 324
Bolivar, Simon, 369
    relations with Mordechai Ricardo, 140, 141
    stay with Curaçao Jewish community, 139
Bordeaux Jews
    relations with Jews in Haiti, Martinique, and Guadeloupe, 415
    trade with Jews in West Indies, 443
Brandon, Samuel, 84
Brazil, Jews in, 462a, 473, 635, 641
Britain, British, 49, 53, 85, 105, 483
    action against St. Eustatius Jews, 175a, 193
    in Barbados, 216, 221
    and Barbados, 217
    in the Caribbean and West Indies, 243, 248, 483, 484
    Jewish colonial settlers' attitude toward authorities, 450
    Jews made denizens in, 597
    Jews originating in West Indies in, 639
    privileges to Jews in Surinam, 77, 78
    relations with Holland (17th c.), 33
    rule in Jamaica, 290a
    South American settlement by, 126
    struggles over colonial rule, 104
burial society, Curaçao, 143
burials, St. Thomas, 331
Burke, Edmund, 175a

C

calendar, events 1914, 17
Carvajal, Luis de, 491, 556
Cardozo, Haham David, 301
Caribbean history, 206, 462, 548
    Jews in, 52, 245, 487
Carigal, Rafael Haim Isaac, 518
    in Barbados, 222
    correspondence with Stiles, 234a
    will of, 229
Castro Tartas, Isaque de, 568, 594, 634
cemetery, 461
    Barbados, 199, 226
    Barranquilla Sephardi, 350
    Belize, 374
    Cap Haitien, 420, 427
    Charlestown (Nevis), 323
    Hunts Bay (Kingston), 286
    Jamaican Jewish, 249, 293
    in Jewish Savanna, 93
    Nevis, 305, 307, 336
    New York Jewish, 502
    Recife, 632
    St. Croix, 312
    St. Eustatius, 180
    St. Thomas, 320, 338
    Savan (Charlotte Amalie), 299, 332
    Savannah (Georgia) Jewish, 553
    Sephardic in South America and West Indies, 475
    Spanish-Portuguese in Philadelphia, 506
Charles II, contract with de Piso, 281
Chile, history of Jews in, 476

chronology, Jewish settlement in Caribbean, 564
circumciser. *See* mohel
cocoa, production of, 37a, 62
Cohen Nassi, David. *See* Nassy
coinage, by Jewish commercial houses, 313, 552
Colon, Portugallo, 257
color, Jews of, 94
commemorations, 456
   anniversary of the Curaçao Mikve Israel synagogue, 161
   anniversary of Joden Savanne synagogue, 37
   of Portuguese Jews in St. Eustatius, 178
   reconsecration of Nevis cemetery, 307
   rededication of St. Thomas synagogue, 304
   restoration of Barbados synagogue, 198
commerce, 102, 313, 443, 452, 464, 474, 488, 552, 572
   Barbados Jews', 216, 221
   British in Barbados and Jamaica, 202a
   Curaçao Jews, 344
   Nevis, 324, 327
   sugar trade and the Jews, 519
community, Jewish
   Barbados, 230
   Curaçao, 133, 156, 176
   Danish West Indies, 337
   Dutch Brazil, families in, 629
   Jamaican, 237, 270, 288
   disputes within, 73a
   Nevis, 310
   Panama, 378
   Portuguese in Caracas, 342
   Recife, 176
   relations between Curaçao and Amsterdam, 155

St. Croix, 298
St. Eustatius, 174, 183, 185, 191, 196
St. Thomas, 298, 302, 322, 328, 485
in Surinam, 54, 60, 69b, 76, 84, 124
in Venezuela, 353
confirmations, St. Thomas, 333
congregation
   Honen Dalim (St. Eustatius), 181, 183
   Kol Shearith Israel, (Panama), 382, 388
   Magen Abraham (Brazil), 507, 628
   St. Thomas, 330
   Temple Kahal Kados Yangakob (Colon), 396
   Zur Israel (Brazil), 507, 628
continuity, Jamaican Jewish, 240
conversos, 490, 491, 567, 568, 570, 611
   and Argentinian history, 612
   in Brazil, 462b, 591, 592, 593, 643, 644
   in Caribbean colonies, 569
   Portuguese, 259, 340, 462a, 554, 623
   in Sao Paulo, 593
   in colonial Latin America, 560, 561, 562, 563
Copiador de Cartas, 585
Cordova, de (fam., Jamaica), 272
Coro, history of Jews in, 359
correspondence, on Jews in Barbados and Jamaica, 465
Costa Rica, history of Jews, 395
Courlanders, Tobago settlement and, 45. *See also* Latvians
crypto-Jews
   Cartagena Inquisition and, 366
   in Mexico, 636, 637

observance of Judaism by, 562
  in Panama, 390, 391
Curaçao, history of Jews in, 135, 136, 137, 138, 146, 148, 161, 162, 163, 164, 165, 171
Curiel (family), 373
Curiel, Elias David, 341, 352, 365, 367
customs, Jewish
  influence on the Surinamese, 87
  of marranos in New World, 562, 563

D

Darkei Yesharim (Jewish community, Paramaribo), 94
De Lima (family), 448
de Lima, Rosa Clara, 445
de Sola (family), 142
de Sola, Juan, 358
decrees and law, on Jews in French Caribbean, 434, 435, 436
Delvalle, Max, 387
demography
  Barbados (17th c.), 214
  Caribbean Jewry, 492
  Jews in Dutch Brazil, 645
Denmark, 300
  rule in St. Thomas, 309, 317a
Depas (family), 425
dictionary, French and Netherlands Antilles colonial terms, 521
discoverers of America, Jewish origin of, 566, 610
discrimination
  Jamaican tax, 251, 252
  social, 16
divorce, West Indies Jews and, 470
documents
  American Jews contacts with the Caribbean, 575
  on Barbados tax on Jews, 228
  British rule in Jamaica, 264
  community membership, St. Thomas, 322, 328
  denization certificate, 281
  on the de Sola family, 142, 159
  on Dutch occupation of the "Wild Coast," 50
  Jewish history in Curaçao, 135
  on Jewish rights, 21, 49, 110
  on Jewish settlement in Pomeroon, 132
  by Jewish settlers from Netherlands, 74
  of Jews in Barbados, 205, 211, 213, 223, 224, 230
  Jews in Dutch Brazil, 630
  on Jews in Jamaica, 213
  on Jews in Remire, 71
  on Jews in Suriname, 18, 46, 53, 51, 101, 107, 109, 110
  Portuguese Jews in France, 83
  on St. Eustatius Jews and the American Revolution, 188
  Tobago, 18, 69
Dominican Republic, history of Jews in, 398, 399, 400, 402, 403
Dutch, the, 55, 100a, 152, 481, 520, 525, 526, 527, 528, 534, 535
  in Brazil, 480
  colonial reports, 99a, 111a, 164a
  colonies in Western Guiana, 85
  colonization of Tobago and the, 45, 48, 55
  in the Guianas, 525, 528
  Jewish congregations in Brazil under, 507, 508
  Jews, 615
  Jews in possessions of, 148, 186
  military campaigns in Suriname, 114, 115
  occupation on the "Wild Coast," 21, 50
  in Remire, 73

Index of Subjects

rules for Portuguese Jews in Curaçao, 169a, 170
settlement in Guiana, 92
settlement in Suriname, 92, 117
Spanish-Poruguese Jews in colonies of the, 478
struggles over colonial rule, 104
and Venezuela, 151
on the Venezuelan coast, 347
in the West Indies, 530
Dutch West India Company, 40, 90

E

economy, 522, 584, 601
  agricultural in South America, 2
  impact of Jews in Holland and Dutch colonies, 622
  Jamaican Jews, 294
  Jewish markets, 11
  Jews in Dutch, 504
education
  Barbados, 203
  Jewish, in Curaçao, 145
  in the Jewish Savanna, 27, 111
Egerton manuscript, 21
Eisenman Brandon, Bob, 375
emissaries, from Holy Land to America, 222, 646
encyclopedias, 509, 510, 511, 512, 513, 535, 540
environment, impact on Jews of, 24
epitaphs, 461
  Barbados Jewish, 199, 226
  monumental in Jewish burial ground, Bridgetown, 233
  from Curaçao's Jewish cemetery, 146, 168, 169
  Danish West Indies, 338
  Jamaican Jewish, 249, 286, 293
  from Jewish Savanna, 56, 91a, 93
  Nevis, 323
  in New York Jewish cemeteries, 502
  St. Croix, 312
  St. Eustatius, 180
  St. Thomas, 320
  in Savannah (Georgia) Jewish cemetery, 553
  West Indies, 595
equality, equal rights
  and Barbados Jews, 232
  and Jamaican Jews, 238, 262, 270
Essequibo River, settlements on, 16
everyday life
  Barbados (17th c.), 202
  Jamaica (17th c.), 202
  Jewish impact on British Caribbean, 581
  Suriname, 5, 47a, 115
exodus, Jews from Brazil, 493, 631
expulsions
  "Black Code," 434, 435
  commemoration of Jews from Spain, 458
  Curaçao Jews from Coro, 346
  Jews from Dutch Brazil, 37a, 642
  Jews from Martinique, 433

F

family life, Jamaican Jewish, 238, 295
family traditions, Sephardi in Latin America, 453
Fidanque (family), 377, 383, 384, 394
France, the French, 119, 275
  Caribbean settlement and, 26, 99
  Cayenne governor at war with Dutch, 100a
  colony in Guiana, 61a, 119
  emissary to Guiana and Martinique, 20a

Jews' activities in colonies of, 37a
Jews under colonial rule of, 11, 413
possessions in Caribbean, 11
religious life in colonies of, 421
settlements in the Caribbean, 417
in struggles over colonial rule, 104, 416
and Tobago, 20
French-Portuguese Jews, 326

G

Gama, Gaspar da, 567
genealogy, 160, 333, 451, 469, 580, 617, 643
    Belinfante family, 201
    Curaçao and Aruba families, 157
    Jewish families from Recife, 619
    Piza family, 565
George (king of England), 450
Gradis (family), 419
graves
    Portuguese Jewish in Hamburg, 219
    Spanish-Portuguese in Philadelphia, 506
gravestones. *See* epitaphs
graveyards. *See* cemeteries
Guadeloupe, history of Jews in, 405

H

Hamilton, Alexander, 319, 334
Hart, Daniel, 446
Hebrew, plantation names in, 59
Henriques Moron (family).
    See Moron
Herrera (family), 370
Holland
    Jews in economy of, 504

relations with England (17th c.), 33
in Western Guiana, 38
Holy Land
    and Haham Carigal, 229
    relations with American Jews, 222
    Suriname Jews' attachment to, 4
Honen Dalim (syn., St. Eustatius), 181, 183
Huguenots, relations with Jews in French West Indies, 440
human rights, U.S.A., 91

I

Inquisition
    Cartagena, 366
    in Colombia, 355
    in colonial Panama, 390
    in Latin America, 613
    in Mexico, 557, 558, 559
    in Portugal, 603
    Portuguese in Brazil, 594
inscriptions. *See* epitaphs
integration, 400
interreligious relations
    Barbados, 203
    in colonial America, 505

J

Jamaica, history, 258, 263, 277
    Jews in, 213, 237, 248, 263, 268, 278, 285, 287, 288, 294
Jerusalem, 4
Jewish life, 569, 588
    Barbados, 210, 211, 212, 224
    in Chile, 477
    in Curaçao, 135, 159
    in Guiana, 9, 61a
    in Jamaica, 242, 280, 292, 295
    in Kingston, 261
    in Martinique, 418, 433, 437
    in Panama under Spanish rule,

Index of Subjects

390, 391
in Peru, 477
in St. Eustatius, 191, 192, 194, 195
in Surinam, 14, 25, 39, 76, 100, 121
Jewish Nation
in Surinam, 25
Jewish religion, prohibition against practicing, 20a
Journals of House of Assembly (Jamaica), 267, 269
Judaism. *See* Jewish religion
jurators, Jewish, 25

K

Karigal, Haijm Isaac. SEE Carigal, Rafael Haim
ketubbah (marriage certificate), 23
Kol Shearith Israel Congregation (Panama), 382, 388

L

La Barre, Antoine Joseph Le Febvre de, 20a
Lampsins brothers, 45
Latvians, Tobago settlement and, 45, 57, 103. *See also* Courlanders
leaders, Jewish, 84, 112, 113, 158, 267, 330
Leon, Moshe de, 84
letters, by Dutch governor of Suriname, 13
Levi de Barrios, David, 67, 80, 98, 543
Lezy, Cyprien Lefebvre de, 100a
Lindo, David, 274
Lindo, Juan, 386
London Times, complaint against Jews, 290a
Lopez (fam.), 160
Lopez, Aaron, 488
Lopez Laguna, Daniel, 244, 270

Lopez-Penha (family), 397, 460, 571
Louis XIV, 434

M

Maduro (family), 497, 552
Mahamad, Spanish and Portuguese Congregation of London, 465
mansions
Curaçao, 167
Suriname Jewish, 118
maps, Surinam, 42, 59
markets
Jewish, 11
Sunday, 324
marranos. *See* conversos
Martinique, history of Jews in, 405
Massiah (fam.), wills of, 212
Mauricius, Jan Jacob (Suriname gov.), 25, 73a
Mendes Chumaceiro (family), 580
Mendes France (family), 406, 441
Mikve Israel (Curaçao), 147
Mikve Israel-Emanuel (Willemstad), 134, 161
Milan, Gabriel, 309, 317a
military units, Jamaican Jewish, 280
mohel, mohelim, 282
in Curaçao and Suriname, 36
Monsanto, David, 84
Montefiore (fam., Barbados), 218
Montefiore, Joshua, 218
Morales, David, 344
Moroccan Jews, in Barcelona (Venezuela), 351
Moron (family), 428
Moron, Simon Henriquez, 429, 431

N

Nacion, La, 454, 458, 625

153

names
  Jewish family, 95
  Hebrew biblical plantation, 59
Nassi. *See* Nassy
Nassy (family), 113
Nassy, David de Isaac Cohen, 13a, 14, 25, 47, 84, 84a, 91, 112
Nevis, history of Jews in, 305, 335
New Christian, settlement in Jamaica, 257
New Orleans, West Indies origin of Jews of, 546
New York, history of Jews in, 603
Nidhei Israel (Bridgetown), 198, 234

O

Obediente (fam.), 236
Obediente, Gideon, 236
Obediente, Joseph, 344
Oppenheim, Samuel, 473
Osorio (family), 385, 392

P

paintings, of Jewish Savanna, 47a, 47b
Panama, history of Jews in, 380, 381
Parra, Ishak de la, 84
Parra, Samuel de la, 84
Paz, Lopez de, 424
Pennsylvania, human rights in, 91
petitions
  Barbados Jews to King William, 213
  by Kingston Jews on charity collection, 267
  St. Eustatius Jews to the British, 193
photographs, 454
  Jewish life in Jamaica, 290
  Spanish-Portuguese communities, 482

physicians, 14, 91, 424
Pimentel (fam.), 160
Pimienta, Jose Diaz, 532
pirates. *See* privateers
Piso, Abraham Israel de, contract with Charles II, 281
Pissarro (fam.), 326, 329
Pissarro, Camille, 326, 329
Piza, Joshua, 565
plantations, 5
  Surinam Jewish, 61
planters, Jewish in Suriname, 114, 115
poets and poetry, 364
  Daniel Levi (Miguel) de Barrios, 67, 80
  Daniel Lopez Laguna, 244, 270
political rights, Suriname Jews', 25
poor, collecting for the Jewish, 267
Portugal, Portuguese
  emissary meeting Portuguese Jews in Suriname and, 4a
  in Jamaica, 264
Portuguese (lang.), Curaçao Jews' use of, 147
Portuguese authorities
  attitude toward Portuguese Jews, 6
  in Brazil and the Jews of Suriname, 6
  letter of appreciation to Suriname Jews, 47
Portuguese Jews, 4a, 6, 275, 348, 358, 387, 451, 514a
  in Barcelona (Venezuela), 351
  in Barranquilla, 355, 366
  in the Caribbean, 539
  community, Barbados (20th c.), 209
  community, Caracas, 342
  community, Suriname, 76
  congregation in Curaçao, 162, 164

154

Index of Subjects

"Copiador de Cartas," 586
Dutch regulations in Curaçao, 169a, 170
marranos in Latin America, 554
in Panama, 375, 376
relations between Hamburg and Barbados, 208, 219
role in press of British Guiana, 105
in St. Eustatius, 178
in Venezuela, 371
prayer
  hymns of Kahal Kados Yangakob, 396
  Suriname Jews' Hebrew, 70
pre-nuptial agreements, 273
press
  British Guiana, 105
printing, Jewish religious books in Jamaica, 250
privateers and pirates, 463
privileges, Suriname Jews', 77, 110

Q
Quakers, Barbados, 203
Quesada, Gonzalo Jimenez de, 363

R
rabbis
  in America, 542
  Suriname, 60
race relations
  in Guiana in colonial times, 87
  Jamaican Jews and, 260
religious leaders
  in Jamaica, 272
  in the Jewish Savanna, 65.
  See also rabbis
religious life, Jewish
  Jamaica, 237, 295
religious problems, Jews settling in Caribbean, 570
responsa, Brazil to Salonika, 614

restorations
  cemetery, 336
  synagogue, 198
Ricardo, Mordechai, 349
  and Bolivar, 140, 141
Ricardo, S. de Jongh, 371
rights, Jewish, 112, 202a
  agreement between Dutch and British on, 49, 531
  Gov. Mauricius and political, 73a
  in Jamaica, 266
  petition from Barbados for, 213
  in Suriname, 110
  on the Wild Coast, 21
riots, anti-Jewish
  Coro, 345, 346, 361
Rivera (fam.), 160
rivers, settlement along, 4, 16
Rodney, Admiral, 175a

S
St. Eustatius Jewish community, history of, 174, 183, 184, 185, 192, 195
Sasportas (fam.), 160
Sasportas, Isaac Yeshurun, 275
Scheltus, Jacob (Dutch printer), 169a
schools, Jewish Savanna, 27, 111
Sephardim, 1, 2, 154, 156, 176, 208, 605, 297, 298, 467
  English, 574
  in Jamaica, 266
  poor in Amsterdam, 22
  in United States, 496
  See also Spanish-Portuguese Jews
Sequera, Juan Lopez, 389
sermons, on rabbis of Curaçao and Barbados, 468
settlement, 16, 26, 92
  Barbados, 203, 217, 220, 223

colonial power struggle for Tobago, 57, 58, 103
Curaçao Jews in Barranquilla, 350
first Jews in Dominican Republic, 402, 403
early European on northern coast of South America, 126
European power struggles over, 106
Portuguese Jews in Barcelona (Venezuela), 351
settlement, Jewish, 4, 74, 88, 89, 90, 138, 176, 621, 627
  in America, 128, 550, 618, 624, 638
  attitudes toward, 73a
  Barbados, 205
  in Brazil, 524
  Brazil Jews on Cayenne, 63
  chronology of Caribbean, 564
  first in Curaçao, 149
  first on American continent, 455, 458, 514, 576
  from France, 83
  in Haiti, 430
  in Jamaica, 246, 257, 259, 266, 270
  in Mexico, 576
  in New Amsterdam, 537, 596, 631, 640
  Pomeroon, 1, 16, 132
  in Remire, 61a, 71, 72
  Spanish-Portuguese in America, 515
  Suriname, 13, 18, 22, 23, 25, 39, 69a, 84, 90a, 98, 101, 107
  Tobago, 3, 18
  under Dutch West India Company, 40
  Virgin Islands, 318
  Western Guiana, 88, 89, 90, 106
  West Indies, 529, 609, 616

Shaare Shalom synagogue (Kingston), 288
sites
  Jewish in Caribbean, 577, 620
  St. Eustatius Jewish, 175, 178, 179
  Suriname Jewish, 96
slave trade, Jews and the, 498
slavery, 5
slaves, 114, 295, 324, 644
social structure, Suriname, 69b
society
  Barbados Jews' position in, 492
  ethnic groups in Jamaican, 241
  Jamaican Jews' role in, 238, 294, 492
  Martinique Jews' position in, 492
Sola, Juan de. SEE de Sola, Juan
soldiers, Jewish, 271, 544, 590
soldiers, Jews as, 544
Sommelsdijck, van Aerssen van, 13
Spanish Jewish Diaspora, 579, 626
Spanish-Portuguese Jews, 459, 465, 471, 482, 496, 618
  centers in Western countries, 587
  in the Caribbean, exhibition, 454
  in Costa Rica, 393
  in Dutch Brazil, 523
  in Dutch Caribbean colonies, 478
  in Dominican Republic, 401, 404
  English in contact with West Indies, 538
  in Guiana, 18
  in Haiti, 425, 429
  history of, 154
  in Jamaica, 254, 267
  in Latin America, 582, 583
  in London, 466
  La Nacion, 454, 458
  in North America, 503

Index of Subjects

in Panama, 381, 382
relations between Amsterdam and Constantinople, 586
settling in America, 515
settling in the West, 541
synagogues in Suriname and Curaçao, 479
in Trinidad, 444, 445, 448
in U.S., 18
in West Indies, 18
See also conversos
Spanish rule in Mexico and Central America, Jews under, 557, 582
stamps, Spanish-Portuguese Jews on, 456, 459
Stiles, Ezra, correspondence with Carigal, 234a
sugar trade, Jews in, 519
Suriname, history
  cartographic, 59
  colonial period, 126
  Jews in, 25, 41, 43, 44, 46, 51, 52, 88, 91a, 107, 109, 245
  settlement, 75
  under British rule, 78
Surinamer (fam.), 95
swearing-in, Jews in courts of Danish West Indies, 300
synagogues
  attack on Speightown, 227, 235
  Bevis Marks, 466
  Bridgetown, 198, 234
  Curaçao, 149, 161, 479
  first American, 489
  inscription of Caribbean, 461
  Jamaican, 237
  Jewish Savanna, 15, 37, 93, 117
  Kingston, 288
  Paramaribo, 15
  Port Royal, 265, 274a
  Recife, 632
  St. Eustatius, 181

St. Thomas, 301
Suriname, 12, 118, 479
Wild Coast, 86
Willemstad, 134

T

taxes, special on Jews, 533
  Barbados, 228
  Jamaica, 251, 252, 269, 283
teaching. *See* education
Tobago, history, 69, 103, 129
tombstones, Jewish Savanna, 64
  See also graves
toponyms, Jewish in Haiti, 426
trade, 216, 601, 602
  West Indies' illicit, 452. *See also* commerce
travel literature, 280
  British woman in St. Eustatius (18th c.), 193a
  Jewish settlers from Netherlands to Pomeroon, 74
  Jewish sites in Suriname, 66
  Labat's description of his voyages, 62, 63
Trevino de Sobremonte, Tomas, 559
tribute, Jews'. *See* taxes
Trinidad, history of, 446, 447, 449

U

United States, first Jews in, 547

V

vanilla production, 62
Vaughan, General, 175a, 197
Venezuela, history of Jews in, 343
Virgin Islands, history of, 303, 318
  Jews in, 296, 298, 325

W

War of Independence, the Jews and the South American, 369

weddings, Jewish in Jamaica, 280
West India Company, 90
West Indies, history of, 549, 578, 602, 605, 606
  Jewish community in, 171, 257, 589
Western Guiana, history of, 106
William III (king), 213
Willoughby (fam.), 217
Willoughby (gov.), 78
wills, 212
  Haham Carigal's, 229
  Jamaican Jewish, 292, 294, 295
  Nevis Jews in New York, 308
  West Indies' Jews, 598
Wolf, Lucien, 599
writers, Jewish
  in America, 542
  Venezuelan, 368

Y

Ylan, Juan de, 158
Yulee, David L., 315

Z

Zemah David (syn., Speightown), attack on, 227, 235
Zionism, early American, 545

Index of Places

Listings for major topics refer only to items not found in their specific sections.

A
Altona, 377, 384
Aruba, 157

B
Barbados, 456, 465, 468, 575, 598
Barcelona (Venezuela), 351
Baromia River, 49
Barranquilla, 350, 355, 366, 397, 451, 571
Belize City, 374
Berbice, 50
Bordeaux, 415
Brazil, 6, 49, 63, 451, 493, 523, 524, 591, 592, 606, 644
Bridgetown, 198, 209, 233
British Guiana, 16, 31
Buenos Aires, 554

C
Cap Haitien, 420, 427
Caracas, 342, 585
Carora (Venezuela), 370, 373
Cartagena, 366
Charlestown (Nevis), 323
Charlotte Amalie, 297, 298, 299, 304, 332
Christiansted (St. Croix), 312
City of David (Panama), 389
Colon (Panama), 396
Coro (Venezuela), 341, 345, 346, 348, 356, 361, 362, 372, 373, 451
Costa Rica, 497, 565

Cuba, 532
Curaçao, 36, 176, 350, 369, 377, 384, 392, 397, 451, 468, 479, 497, 518, 526, 532, 565, 571, 575, 580, 586

D
Demerary, 16, 50, 99a, 111a

E
Essequibo, 50, 99a, 111a

G
Grand'Anse, 429, 430, 431
Guiana, Western, 31, 37, 88, 89
Guyana (Guiana), 9, 18, 20a, 61a, 525, 528

H
Haiti. *See* Saint Domingue
Hamburg, 208, 377, 384
  Portuguese Jewish graves in, 219

I
Irmire. *See* Remire
Izmir, 397, 571

J
Jamaica, 201, 202, 213, 465, 575, 598, 606
Jewish Savanna, 15, 27, 28, 29, 30, 37, 47a, 47b, 56, 60, 61, 64, 65, 93, 96, 111, 117

159

K
Kingston, 241, 261, 267

L
London, 201
  Jewish soldiers in, 271
  Obediente family in, 236

M
Maracaibo, 571
Martinique, 11, 20a, 37a, 98, 575
Mexico, 555, 556, 557, 558, 623, 637
Moron, 428

N
Netherlands Antilles, 456, 526, 527, 535
Nevis, 236, 598
New Orleans, 546
New York, 308, 471, 502, 603
New Zealand (Pomeroon), 88
Newport (Rhode Island), 138, 234a, 518

O
Olinda, 508, 628

P
Panama, 456, 497, 565, 580
Paramaribo, 15, 94
Pauroma. *See* Pomeroon
Philadelphia, 14, 91, 506
Pomeroon, 1, 16, 49, 74, 132
Port of Spain, 445, 448
Port Royal (Jamaica), 242, 265, 274a
Portugal, 6

R
Recife, 176, 508, 628
Remire, 61a, 73

S
Saint Domingue, 411, 424, 430, 431, 432
Saint Eustatius, 585
St. Michael, 284
St. Thomas, 297, 298, 377, 384, 392, 565
Santo Domingo, 397, 398, 402, 403, 404, 571
Sao Paulo, 592
Speightown (Barbados), 227, 235
Suriname River, 4
Suriname, 245, 456, 479, 501, 526, 527, 575, 585, 606

T
Tobago, 3, 19, 20
Trinidad, 19
Tucacas (Venezuela), 138, 347

U
United States, 18, 496,

V
Venezuela, 138, 151, 456, 580
Vermont, 218

W
West Indies, 49, 416, 417, 452
  British, 18
  Danish, 300, 337
  Dutch, 18
  French, 440
Wild Coast, 21, 50, 86, 114